Great Stories Behind Famous Books

Don L. Wulffson

Alleyside Press ®

Fort Atkinson, Wisconsin

*To the Dedicated Teachers & Librarians
of Los Angeles*

Published by Alleyside Press, an imprint of Highsmith Press
W5527 Highway 106
P.O. Box 800
Fort Atkinson, Wisconsin 53538-0800   **1-800-558-2110**

© Don L. Wulffson, 1999
Cover design: Frank Neu

The paper used in this publication meets the minimum requirements of American National Standard for Information Science — Permanence of Paper for Printed Library Material. ANSI/NISO Z39.48-1992.

Library of Congress Cataloging-in-Publication Data
        Wulffson, Don L.
            Great stories behind famous books / Don L. Wulffson.
                p.   cm.
            Includes bibliographical references.
            ISBN 1-57950-033-1 (softcover : alk. paper)
            1. Literature–Study and teaching (Secondary) 2. Teenagers–Books
        and reading. 3. Authors–Biography. II. Title.
        PN59.W85 1999
        807'. 1' 2–dc21
                                                                 99-35478
                                                                    CIP

Contents

[Exercise sheet ▢] This notation is used in the Teacher Resources sections to indicate activities that include a printed student exercise in the Student Assignment.

Introduction

Children learn best when they are active rather than passive participants; learning is genuinely fun and rewarding when children are fully engaged in the learning process; all educational strategies, goals, and materials are subordinate to the aptitudes, perceptions, and experiences the child brings to the classroom. This is Whole Language learning, and it is this approach to education upon which this work is based.

Great Stories Behind Famous Books introduces young people to the fascinating lives, happenings, and vicissitudes of circumstance and timing which combined to produce some of the world's greatest literature. In conjunction with these selections, utilizing a holistic format, the student is presented with a rich multiplicity of learning activities which touch upon the entire spectrum of secondary language arts—critical thinking, reading comprehension, word and vocabulary development, writing, and research skills.

While providing structural continuity in its presentation, the work nonetheless proffers activities which are unusual, even unorthodox and surprising, with the intent of constantly finding new means of stimulating any and all cognitive and affective dimensions of the learner. To this end, integrated into this work are cooperative (team) learning strategies, competitive strategies, and various techniques which allow the student to assume the role, function, and responsibilities of a teacher. At the same time, not excluded by any means are traditionalist modes and materials of proven worth.

Careful attention has been paid to the choosing of those writers and works which are presented. The essential criteria include: 1) Each work must be a classic, a book of time-tested literary (and social) merit; 2) Each title must have very strong name recognition, and young people should be familiar with the contents of the work (via exposure to one or more media); 3) Every work is of a kind we can anticipate would be an acceptable part of the curriculum of any secondary school and readily available at local school and public libraries; 4) As a whole, the works provide a represen-tative spectrum of genre—including science fiction, mystery, horror, fantasy, romance, poetry, and non-fiction; 4) Finally, the reading of the biographical selection should serve as a stimulus and springboard into the reading of a variety of works by the author.

As teachers/librarians we know that there are few experiences more exciting and fulfilling than true learning, unless it is to provide for children this self-same experience. We teach a little of knowledge, a bit of information; but true teaching occurs when the student learns how to learn, and discovers that he or she loves to learn. This book, then, is one vehicle in pursuance of this seemingly lofty—but very realistic and attainable—goal.

How to Use This Book

This book is intended for use by senior or junior high school teachers or librarians for strengthening student reading comprehension, and stimulating reading interest. It can also be used in public libraries by young adult librarians for teen book discussion groups or after-school activities. The chapter that follows (p. 6) describes how to develop a teen book discussion group.

Each unit consists of a reading selection followed by student activities and teaching material. The teaching material describes the objectives of the student activities and provides additional techniques and procedures to be used in conjunction with the reading selection. For the teacher, the material is divided into Before Reading Activities, During Reading Activities, and After Reading Activities.

The reading selection and student material may be photocopied for immediate use as classwork and/or homework. When there is a printed activity in the student section, this is indicated in the teacher resources with the following: [Exercise sheet ☐].

Generally, the activities are presented in the following sequence: critical & analytical thinking, word/language skills, written expression (with an emphasis on creative writing), and library/information-seeking skills.

Starting a Book Discussion Group for Teens

by Donna McMillen

Book groups for teens can be an effective way to encourage reading among teens who are already readers, and to help develop reading skills in those who might not choose reading first as an activity. Book groups are springing up all over—in libraries, in schools, in homes, in homeschool groups, and in bookstores. Starting a book group involves decisions—about the focus of the group, finding the books, publicity, scheduling, location, age of the participants, and size of group. Caroline Ward gives "The ABCs of Book Discussions" in her article "Having Their Say." (*School Library Journal*, April 1998, p. 27) A variety of book discussion groups for teens have been successful, according to numerous printed references.

Organizing the Group and Finding the Books

Groups can be focused on the classics, on contemporary books, on a genre, on mother/daughter topics, or on favorites chosen by the group. For three years I have successfully organized a group for ages twelve to eighteen to discuss the nominees for the Best Books for Young Adults (American Library Association). Mother/daughter groups have been popular since the publication of Shireen Dodson's *The Mother Daughter Book Club*. There are many guides available to help a leader or group choose books that will generate good discussions. Try some of the resources in the attached bibliography or ask at your local library or bookstore. The leader may choose all the books or choose only the first one, then have group members choose the books to follow. Try starting with one of the books highlighted in this volume, using the background story as a discussion starter. One idea for high school students might be to read some of these classics as a college preparation exercise. Reading older titles or books out in paperback may be easier than trying to get enough copies of the latest hardback bestseller.

Will the leader provide enough copies of the book or will readers need to find them themselves? Will the books be borrowed from libraries (do they have book group sets?), or perhaps donated by a PTA group or Friends of the Library or sponsored by a grant from a civic group or other local organization? Will the local bookstore offer a discount for multiple copies? Will the group read and discuss one title, or will they function as a review group, sharing titles they have been reading since the last meeting? If it will be a review group, consider having a focus for each meeting, such as a genre, a time period, or award-winning books. Some review groups concentrate on "new" books or may even have advance reading copies from publishers. A book discussion group might set aside time to mention other books that members may be reading, after the main book is discussed.

Planning for Publicity

Create a publicity plan. Contact teens you know who would be interested in discussing books and have them invite their friends to the first meeting. Contact teachers and school librarians to have them personally give invitations/flyers to teen readers. Parents will be encouraged to transport their teen if they see the publicity. (A teen once told me she could get her mom to bring her to the library for the regular book group meeting, but not so easily for other activities.) Send an announcement to the PTA for their newsletter at the schools for your target age group. Visit classrooms to talk about books and promote the book group. Send flyers to all the language arts teachers. Give a blurb to the school to be read with the morning announcements. Advertise in the library and school library with a catchy poster and program title. Advertise in the school paper. Make it upbeat and fun—mention refreshments! Start a registration list and do reminder calls a few days before the program—teens are busy and even the most enthusiastic may forget about the meeting. Keep the advertising ongoing to encourage more teens to join in and be sure that new members are made welcome to keep them coming back. The group may start small and grow as word of mouth spreads. Encourage regulars to bring guests!

When and Where?

When will the meetings be held and how often? Most book groups find the once a month format works well during the school year. Teens may have a hard time finding enough non-homework time to read a book if the meetings are more often. Summer groups can successfully meet more often, though members may occasionally be gone for vacations. Summer is a good time for many teens to do lots of reading! Decide what time of day to meet—midmorning (in the summer), after school, afternoon, evening or weekend? Do the potential members come from one school making an afterschool meeting feasible? Do members live within walking distance or will they have to come by auto from all over, making an evening meeting a better choice? Plan on an hour, though meetings can run shorter, especially the first few times. If this group is part of your work, how will it fit into your schedule? How long will this series of meetings run—school year, semester, summer, five meetings? Where will the group meet—library, school, homes, community building, coffeehouse, book store? Find a setting that will encourage discussion (few interruptions and comfortable seating) and where refreshments will be okay.

Who to Include

What ages will this group take in? Some groups successfully accommodate a wider range of ages, but you may want to decide if this will be a junior high or senior high group. Senior high students are busier, but may be able to transport themselves, while junior high students may be relying on parents for transportation. My combined age book group gets a reminder at the beginning that all opinions are to be respected and that different books appeal to different people and even to the same person at different ages. If you do have an age limit, keep a list of teens to contact when they reach the age you've set—they will probably still be interested next year. In addition, think about the size of the group—six to fifteen participants is ideal, though a group can function with fewer or more. My summer series has up to twenty sign up, with ten to fifteen attending each session, while the fall series has fewer sign-ups, but more regular attendance. Do you want to limit the number or take all comers? If the group is too large and unwieldy, consider dividing into a couple of groups, giving more

options for time of meetings or age grouping. An existing group may "grow" out of existence as the seniors all graduate, unless new younger members have been added all along!

Setting Up the Meeting

Now that the meeting is set, how do you get started? Use one of the written activities in this book, such as a word scramble, as an icebreaker. Have entering students work in pairs to try to unscramble the words while waiting for others to come in. Have refreshments set out—they are a nice icebreaker, give people something to do with their hands, and create a feeling of comfortable casualness. Pizza is always popular with teens, but cookies, fruit, nuts, soda, hot chocolate, chips and dip, snack crackers, or popcorn are other possibilities. It is a good idea to have non-caffeinated beverages and non-sugar snack options available, for those who need or prefer them. Greet each person as they come in and encourage them to settle in with a name tag, refreshments, introductions, handouts, and any icebreaker activity you've planned. Have a registration sheet set up. Have a display of new and interesting books for early comers to browse. The early arrivals can help you with final set up details—a great way to incorporate their help and break the ice too!

During the Meeting

When you're ready to start, begin with an around-the-room introduction by having each person give their name, school, and one fact about themselves, such as their favorite recent movie, number and type of pets, or favorite singer. Give a brief explanation of the purpose of the group and give the basic rules of discussion, such as respecting the opinions of others, listening to the person speaking, positive comments first, not giving away the ending of a book that others have not read, and giving all a chance to talk.

Give a book talk to start, or play a selection from a book on tape, or read (or play a taped reading) of one of the stories from this volume to get the group warmed up. Have some leading questions prepared if the group has already all read one book, chosen and advertised ahead of time. (What kind of person is the main character? How does the setting contribute to the story?) Have some general discussion questions prepared if each person will be talking about different books. (What was most memorable about the book? Why would you recommend this book to others, or why not?)

Some leaders will want to share interesting facts about the author or time period of the book to be discussed. Recruit a teen ahead of time to start the discussion. If it looks like the group is going to be tongue tied, have a supply of mini candy bars to toss to anyone who contributes anything to the discussion—chocolate works wonders! As the discussion moves along, the leader may need to lead the discussion back to the book if the group gets sidetracked too far.

If the group will be choosing books for later meetings, have a number of possibilities ready for them to look at and give a brief book talk for each, then have the group discuss which books they would like to read for the following meetings. Will a group member take responsibility for introducing the book next time, or will the leader/organizer be doing this? As a second icebreaker, or to discover possible discussion books, or as a wrap-up, have each person tell briefly about a favorite recently read book.

Make arrangements to have copies of the next book available. How will the group members be able to pick up their copies and when? Let the group know you will be doing reminder calls before the next meeting (or sending out postcards.) When you are ready to end the meeting, find a natural stopping point and wrap it up—don't let the discussion just dwindle away. It is better to end a bit early than to have a dragged-out ending. As the meeting breaks up, encourage people to linger over refreshments and the book display. Have the handouts set out, perhaps including some interesting booklists and/or bookmarks. Encourage help with the clearing up! It will help you to get to know the teens as well as being a good way for them to participate as a volunteer.

Additional Activities

For additional activities, you may want to consider having the group think about doing a newsletter of reviews and other book-related topics, or publishing reviews or lists of favorite teen books in a local paper or in the school paper. Members could create a website or send reviews to an existing website for teens or books. Book group members could also take a "field trip" to a play, author visit, or bookstore. Try bringing in a guest speaker for part of a meeting.

If the group is part of a library setting, consider having them go along to help purchase some paperbacks for the library collection. Let the group have first chance at the new books for the library or help with processing paperbacks for checkout. Some group members may want to volunteer to help at the local library's Friends of the Library book sale. Book donations could be gathered to give to needy groups at holiday time, or for a gift tree, or to give to a book sale. The group could participate in or sponsor a writing or poetry contest, or a "design-your-own" book cover contest. Extra activities during National Library Week in April or Teen Read Week in October could be considered. We've had a pizza party with another Best Books for Young Adults group in the area, along with a drawing in which everyone gets a book (advance or review copies and other donations) for our final summer meeting.

Above all, have fun! Being part of a book group can be one of the most enjoyable activities for a teen, as well as for the leader!

Bibliography

Borders, Sarah G., and Alice Phoebe Naylor. *Children Talking About Books.* Oryx, 1993.

Clark, Mary, and Kate McClelland. "Young Critics with a Passion for Books," *BookLinks,* July 1997, p. 23+.

"Dear Author: Students Write about the Books that Changed Their Lives." Collected by the *Weekly Reader's Read* magazine. Berkeley: Conari Press, 1995.

Dodson, Shireen. *The Mother-Daughter Book Club: How Ten Busy Mothers and Daughters Came Together to Talk, Laugh, and Learn Through Their Love Reading.* HarperCollins, 1997.

Jacobsohn, Rachel W. *The Reading Group Handbook: Everything You Need to Know to Start Your Own Book Club.* Hyperion, 1998.

Langer, Lois, Mary Weber, and Wendy Woodfill. "Children's Book Discussion Groups," *Public Libraries,* November/December 1993, p. 315-7.

Laskin, David, and Holly Hughes. *The Reading Group Book: The Complete Guide to Starting and Sustaining a Reading Group with Annotated Lists of 250 Titles for Provocative Discussion.* Plume, 1995.

Madison, Katie O'Dell. "Books, Bytes, & Bucks: Library Prep for the College Bound." *VOYA,* October 1998, p. 258+.

Ward, Caroline. "Having Their Say: How to Lead Great Book Discussions with Children." *School Library Journal,* April 1998, p. 24+.

Websites

Multnomah County Library Kids Page, Mother Daughter Book Group

www.multnomah.lib.or.us/lib/kids/mdbg.html

Mother/daughter book discussion group reading choices and how-to tips

Penguin Putnam Inc. Online

www.penguinputnam.com/clubppi/index.htm

Go to Reading Group and to Teacher's Guides under Academic Arena for a list of online reader's guides to print out.

Random House Library Services, Book Discussion Guides

www.randomhouse.com/library/rgg.html

Look under Reading Group Guides for a variety of guides to print

Rutgers University, Literary Resources on the Net

http://andromeda.rutgers.edu/~jlynch/Lit/

Links to multiple sites for literature

TeenHoopla: An Internet Guide for Teens, Literature

http://www.ala.org/teenhoopla/homework.html

Select Literary Resources for the High School and College Student

Many other publishers offer reading group discussion guides—write to the publisher or look at their website for a list of guides offered. Try library, school and college websites for additional literary resources, or use a search engine to find specific authors.

Chapter 1

Madman on an Island

Defoe's Robinson Crusoe

It is unlikely that you are acquainted with the names Daniel Foe and Alexander Selcraig. However, both men led rather extraordinary lives. And both played a part in the birth of one of the most famous novels ever written.

Alexander Selcraig

Let's start with Alexander Selcraig. Born in 1676 in Largo, Scotland, Selcraig was a surly, hot-tempered teenager who was constantly in trouble with his family and the local authorities. By the time he was nineteen, his most notable accomplishment had been to be forced to leave town for attacking other boys in the middle of church services. He became a sailor and spent six years at sea. Upon returning home, he beat up his father and several of his brothers during a family dispute.

Changing his name from Selcraig to Selkirk, he shipped out aboard a privateer. Off the coast of South America, Selkirk's vessel engaged two Spanish galleons in battle. It was badly shot up, but it limped away and anchored off the remote island of Juan Fernandez to make emergency repairs.

When the captain was ready to leave again, Selkirk was not. The sailor said he would rather be put ashore on the desolate little island than continue in a leaking ship with an imbecile for a captain. The captain was more than willing to oblige the disrespectful young man. At the last minute, Selkirk changed his mind. Weeping, he waded into the surf and begged to be taken back. From the deck, the captain laughed and sailed away.

Alone on the island, with only a rifle, a knife, and a small sea chest, Selkirk was terrified. He spent his first nights shivering in trees, afraid of rats and other animals that roamed the ground. Later, he built a crude shelter, and spent the days hunting for shellfish and eating them raw. Venturing inland, he found that hundreds of cats and goats abounded on the island. Like the rats, several had been left behind two centuries before by the island's discoverer, Juan Fernandez, and the animals had procreated steadily.

Selkirk moved into a cave. There, he tamed wild cats, and with them, he kept up an ongoing battle with the hordes of rats on the island. By day, he hunted goats, and became so fleet of foot—and so bestial—he could run the animals down and kill them with his bare hands.

As time passed and his clothes rotted off, Selkirk replaced them with a bizarre goat hide costume. Now and then, he read the Bible, his only book. He talked to his cats, for dozens of them lived with him in the cave. He talked to himself. He sang. He cried. He screamed. Gradually, with no human company, Selkirk was all but insane.

After more than four years, Selkirk was finally rescued by two British ships driven to the island by a storm. The English sailors found him to be half man, half beast, and almost completely out of his mind. He babbled incoherently, having temporarily lost the ability to speak.

Little by little, he recovered his sanity—at least to a degree, and eventually returned to Scotland. Strange, nervous, awkward, eccentric—he was these things, and more. On his family's property, he dug a cave into the side of a hill; and he lived in there with only a blanket and a few necessities. His only

From *Great Stories Behind Famous Books*. Copyright © 1999 by Don L. Wulffson. (Alleyside Press, 1999)

friends were cats; he tamed local strays, and lived with them, and taught them to do little tricks and dances. Now and then, dressed in rags, he ventured out of his cave, and into town. He mostly kept to himself, but on occasion he would tell others the story of his nightmarish ordeal on the island.

Daniel Foe

Now we come to the other man mentioned earlier. At various times in his life, Daniel Foe had been a merchant, an insurance agent, a brick maker, and a writer of stories and political pamphlets. All his business ventures failed. For his writings, which criticized the government, he spent many years in jail. In 1705, to establish a new identity, Foe changed his name to Defoe.

By chance, one day Defoe happened to hear the story of Selkirk, the strange castaway of Juan Fernandez. It is believed—but not known for certain—that he visited Largo, Scotland, to get a first-hand account from the man himself. Regardless, the story fired Defoe's imagination. He sat down and, with a quill pen and ink, began to write a novel. Changing the name of the story's protagonist, he titled his work *The Adventures of Robinson Crusoe.*

Unlike Selkirk, Crusoe was marooned on the island due to a shipwreck. Though lonely, he did not hide in trees or babble to himself. He triumphed over nature—he built a home for himself; he grew food; he domesticated goats to supply himself with milk, cheese, and meat; he devised a kiln for making crockery and an oven for cooking bread. In almost every endeavor, he was both ingenious and successful. When rescued, he was not a whimpering, dirty beast. Through his ordeal, he had remained a dignified and civilized human being.

Like so many other works, *Robinson Crusoe* is fiction based on a real occurrence. It all started when an ill-tempered sailor rashly demanded to be put ashore on a remote island. A penniless writer heard of the tale and, changing and adding details to suit himself, he produced a work that is both powerful and timeless.

Student Assignment

Fluent and Flexible Thinking

1. Imagine you are going to be living alone for three months in a secluded wilderness, a place with a moderate temperature and ample water. There is a lake, and fish and game. You can take only six items with you, none of them electronic. List the six things you would take that you consider most essential to your survival.

2. In what ways, if any, does living alone appeal to you?

3. In what ways, if any, does living alone not appeal to you?

4. Study your answer to question number 1. Which was the best choice you made? Explain. Which was the poorest? For the poorest of your choices, explain one thing you wish you had taken instead.

Word Analysis: Denotation and Connotation

A word's denotation may be thought of as its dictionary meaning, its core of meaning. But a word suggests or calls to mind many things—memories, feelings, and both universal and personal associations. For example, the word *red*, besides its core meaning, connotes anger, sunburn, fire, blood, and so forth. For each of the following words, give at least three things it connotes. (If necessary, look up the denotation.)

1. sailor

2. cave

3. rot

4. kiln

5. church

6. famous

7. costume

8. emergency

9. galleon

10. eccentric

Cooperative Learning

On a separate sheet of paper, write ten questions of a factual nature about the story. (They may be multiple-choice, complete answer, true-false, etc.) When you finish, exchange papers with another student, and answer the questions, writing:

Answered by _(your name)_____

at the bottom of the paper. Exchange papers again; correct each other's work, then turn it in to the teacher.

Reading for Detail

The following is an abridgment of the opening of chapter 6 of *Robinson Crusoe*. Is there a flaw in the narrative? If so, what is it?

A little after noon I found the sea very calm and I resolved to get to the ship where it was wedged in the rocks. I pulled off my clothes and swam out to the vessel, and spotting a thick rope dangling to the level of the water, managed to climb this to the forecastle of the ship. To my great joy I found that the ship's provisions were dry, and being well-disposed to eat, I went to the bread-room and filled my pockets with biscuits and ate some of them as I searched about me. Now I wanted to find a boat to carry the items from the wreck which I foresaw would be very necessary to me.

Study Defoe's original version of chapter 6 ("I Furnish Myself with Many Things"). Compare it with the abridged version above in terms of: (1) style, (2) detail, (3) word choice, (4) sentence structure, (5) punctuation, (6) clarity.

Language Skills Development: Similes and Metaphors

A simile is a comparison using the words *like* or *as*, while a metaphor does not employ these words. Complete the following sentences to create similes.

1. The setting sun made the sea look

   _____

   _____

   _____.

2. Fog drifted across the land

   _____

   _____

   _____.

3. The fog crept slowly through the jungle vegetation

   _____

   _____

   _____.

4. The sky was as _____ as

   _____

   _____.

From *Great Stories Behind Famous Books*. Copyright © 1999 by Don L. Wulffson. (Alleyside Press, 1999)

5. The broken wood guardrail dangled over the side of the ship. Its spindles

_____

_____

_____.

Turn each of the above similes into metaphors. In most cases this can be accomplished simply by removing the words *like* and *as*.

Narrative Writing

Write a journal in which you are stranded on an island. Begin with the following.

> **Day 1:** I awoke tangled in debris on the sand, battered and bloody and shivering from the cold. Struggling to all fours, I looked out to sea, where the stern of the schooner lay smashed upon some rocks. During the night it had broken in half, and nowhere was there a trace of the bow. Turning, I saw a body lying on the sand. I assumed the person was dead, but…

Library and Information-Seeking Skills

1. Locate the island of Juan Fernandez off the coast of South America, checking several sources to find the largest map available. Make your own copy. How far is the nearest continent? Using atlases, weather and climate charts, or online sources, find out what the climate is like for that part of the world. In what ways would the climate affect Crusoe's ability to survive? What current information did you find about the island, including population?

2. Other stories of survival are *The Swiss Family Robinson* by Johann Wyss, *The Wreck of the Barque Stefano off the North West Cape of Australia in 1875* by Gustave Rathe, *Shipwreck at the Bottom of the World* by Jennifer Armstrong, and *The Upside-Down Ship* by Don L. Wulffson. Use the library catalog or an online source such as <www.amazon.com> to find other stories of survival. Find one of these books and compare the story to that of Robinson Crusoe? In what ways is the story similar and in what ways does it differ? Is the story fiction or nonfiction? Write your results in a brief paragraph. Include the author and title of the book you chose.

Teacher Resources
Whole Language Activities for "Madman on an Island"

Before Reading Activities

Introducing the Student to the Book

The title *Great Stories Behind Famous Books* is self-explanatory. However, reinforce the students' understanding by explaining that there is always a story behind every work of literature they read, and that these stories are often as interesting as the works themselves. Explain that all the works dealt with in the text are classics, and those selected were ones with especially unique and interesting stories behind them. As they read "Madman On an Island," ask them to consider the question: What makes a book a classic?

Fluent and Flexible Thinking [Exercise sheet ☐]

This activity encourages the students to identify with the situation of the protagonist of the selection. For item number 1, call on two or three students to read off their lists. Ask the class to note both similarities and differences in the lists. Also, ask them to discuss the item they now consider a poor choice, and their reasons for reconsideration. Brainstorm with them regarding questions 2 and 3, writing down the _Advantages_ and _Disadvantages_ of living alone on the board.

Word Analysis: Denotation and Connotation
[Exercise sheet ☐]

Throughout this work, it is essential to stimulate an increase in the student's awareness of the multiple effects of individual words and of language as a whole upon the reader. This includes, of course, the generally affective and associative referents of connotation.

During Reading Activities

1. Read the entire selection aloud to the students. This should pique their interest. Do not assume all the students will read the selection on their own or fully understand it.

2. Now have students read the selection silently. As they do, have them list the similarities and differences between Defoe and Selkirk as people.

After Reading Activities

Comparative Thinking

Write _Similarities_ and _Differences_ on the board. Brainstorm with the students; and write down the ways the students see Defoe and Selkirk as alike and different.

Cooperative Learning [Exercise sheet ☐]

Students need to interact with each other as well as the teacher and the materials presented. Have each student write questions (multiple choice, fill-in-the-blank, or true/false). When each finishes, he exchanges papers with another student, answers the questions, and puts:

Answered by _____

at the bottom of the paper. The papers are then again exchanged and the students correct each other's work.

Reading for Detail [Exercise sheet ☐]

It is essential to student growth as readers that they examine written works with a keen and analytic eye. In the excerpt, Crusoe takes off his clothes, swims to the wreck, then puts biscuits in his pocket.

Secondly, make photocopies and a transparency of Defoe's original (the opening of chapter 6), and distribute the copies to the students. As they compare the original with the abridged version, they once again have a basis for careful examination of a work, now in terms of style, sentence structure, word choice, etc.

Language Skills Development: Similes and
Metaphors [Exercise sheet ☐]

Through this activity, students can learn to recognize similes and metaphors and to apply them to their writing. Call on students to read some of their answers aloud. To ensure that students understand the difference between simile and metaphor, make a transparency of the assignment. Then work aloud with the class in changing the similes into metaphors.

Narrative Writing [Exercise sheet ☐]

Before the students begin to write, brainstorm with them. First, have them read the directions for completing the assignment. Then pose each of the following questions, and write down all the responses on the board.

Questions:

1. What are some of the things you might see on the island?

2. What are some of the things you might hear? Smell? Taste? Feel?

3. What are some of the things that might happen?

4. What are some of the things you might do?

Analytical Thinking

Brainstorm with the students as to what qualifies a book as a classic. Write all the students' suggestions on the board. Possible answers: a unique story; the first of its kind; universal appeal—to all sorts of people, not just a small group; of the highest quality; of enduring, time-tested worth.

As to the question of *Robinson Crusoe's* status as a classic, possible answers may include: the theme of man versus nature had never before been dealt with in such an interesting and dramatic way; at the same time, it shows man living in harmony with nature; it appeals to our desire to be alone and to live simply and unfettered by the constraints of society; it appeals to our desire to think creatively, think "for ourselves," and to adapt to a difficult situation in order to survive.

Library and Information-Seeking Skills
[Exercise sheet ☐]

The purpose of these questions and activities is to familiarize students with current print and electronic resources available in the school or public library, and information that is accessible on the Internet.

1. Recommend that the students use a gazetteer to identify the geographic area, and an atlas to locate the specific island.

2. Encourage the students to use *The Readers' Advisor.* However, extensive references are available on the Web using the titles and authors as search terms.

Chapter 2

A Person in Two

Stevenson's *Dr. Jekyll & Mr. Hyde*

One morning in 1885 an ailing Robert Louis Stevenson locked himself in his study to write. Three days later he emerged, pale and gaunt. He had in hand the completed manuscript of *The Strange Case of Dr. Jekyll and Mr. Hyde.*

The story is both brilliant and terrifying. It tells of a good man, Dr. Jekyll, who concocts a potion that can turn him into a monstrous, thoroughly evil man, Mr. Hyde. After Jekyll is transformed into Hyde, he prowls city streets at night, stealing and murdering. At dawn he downs the contents of a second vial and reverts back to the good Dr. Jekyll.

The real-life figure who inspired this story was a Scottish deacon and cabinetmaker named William Brodie. Brodie was born in 1741 and died by hanging in 1788. In his adult years, Brodie lived an incredible dual existence. By day he was a respected businessman and city official, lauded by others for his kindness, intelligence, and good works. By night he was a crude, bestial thief, a violent man with a sadistic penchant for hurting others. As a child, Robert Louis Stevenson read about Brodie and became obsessed with the story. Stevenson grew up in Edinburgh, Scotland, where a street is named after Brodie. And in Stevenson's bedroom stood a rather ornate, handmade cabinet produced by the good-evil man. Stevenson was all too familiar with the dark, sinister tales suggested by that piece of furniture.

At the age of 15, Stevenson wrote a drama called *Deacon Brodie*, an interesting work, but one that was rather simplistic in its execution. Years later he rewrote the play; and it was produced, with some success, in London. Still, Stevenson was not satisfied that he had made the best use of the material. He did not feel he had fully developed his theme—that is, in all people, there is both good and evil, and that most of us hide the dark side of our selves and, generally, keep it under control.

One night in 1885, Stevenson awoke from a horrible nightmare. In it, a handsome gentleman approaches; as he does, he grabs hold of his face, and tearing off the flesh, reveals a second countenance beneath, that of a hideous, vile being. As Stevenson rose from his bed and paced the floor, the plot of *Dr. Jekyll and Mr. Hyde* took form in his mind.

In Stevenson's tale, Dr. Jekyll is driven by curiosity to explore the dark side of his nature. He uses drugs to change from one personage to the other. Brodie, on the other hand, was not driven by curiosity, but by greed and a strange dual personality.

By day, Brodie was a perfect gentleman—well-educated, polite, refined. With nightfall, he assumed another guise; shunning his society friends, he kept company with crude characters in the worst parts of town. He gambled with loaded dice and marked cards. He drank heavily, used obscene language, and caroused with loose women.

To make extra cash, Brodie plunged into thievery. At first he worked alone. Donning a mask and dressed all in white (unlike Stevenson's fictional Mr. Hyde, who wore black), Brodie began burglarizing houses. It was especially amusing, he thought, to steal from his neighbors and good friends, and delighted in taking their most prized possessions, defiling their homes, and causing them great personal distress. Later, Brodie organized a gang of thieves. Soon, a series of daring robberies had the entire citizenry of Edinburgh in a state of anxious consternation.

Brodie met his downfall one frigid, windy night in March of 1788. Surprised during a robbery attempt, he fled in a panic, leaving the rest of his gang behind. Angry at having been deserted, one member informed the police of Brodie's identity. With detectives hot on his heels, Brodie fled to Europe. He was found hiding in a cupboard in a house in Amsterdam, Holland.

Brought home to Edinburgh, Brodie was given a quick trial, found guilty, and sentenced to hang. He was taken to a cell and chained to the floor. On his last morning he walked cheerfully to the gallows. He thought he had nothing to fear because he had

devised an elaborate scheme to save himself. He had slid a silver tube into his throat to keep the noose from closing his windpipe; he had bribed the hangman to make the rope short so that his neck would not be broken by a long drop; and he had hired a French surgeon to revive him.

After the drop, Brodie was cut down and whisked away by friends to the surgeon. But the doctor could not revive him; William Brodie was dead.

Almost a hundred years passed before Brodie could be revived. Only a man as gifted as Robert Louis Stevenson could have done it. Using the dual form of Dr. Jekyll and Mr. Hyde, the famous author returned Brodie to the world of the living.

Student Assignment

Reading Techniques

1. Skim read the entire selection, taking no more than 30 seconds to do so.

2. Read the selection silently and carefully.

3. Skim read the selection again. As you do, write down three things you did not know before reading it.

Analyzing the Structure of a Piece of Writing

1. Study the second paragraph of the selection? What is its purpose?

2. Brodie expected to survive the hanging. However, when, in the third to the last paragraph, you read that "he walked cheerfully to the gallows," you know that he will _not_ survive. Why do you know this?

3. What is the purpose of the next-to-last paragraph?

4. What is the purpose of the last paragraph?

Understanding Theme

1. Divide a piece of paper in half (but do not give your name). On the left side of the paper, write the word "good," then write down one personal quality of yours which you feel is good (e.g., kind to animals). On the right side of your paper, write the word "bad," then write down one personal quality or characteristic you feel is negative (e.g., sarcastic). Without giving names, the teacher will then read the responses aloud to the class.

2. Are all of us a mix of good and bad? Explain. Give examples from real life.

3. Is it simplistic to identify any quality or characteristic as entirely bad? For example, look at the

characteristic you identified as "bad" in question number 1. Is there anything "good" about the quality you listed? For example, is being sarcastic an entirely bad quality? Discuss this.

4. As homework, play a few songs. Find one which expresses one of the following motifs (or a similar motif): (a) Love is both happy and sad; (b) People are often "two-faced"; (c) There is a "dark side" to all people; (d) Even the worst of people have something good about them. Write a one paragraph description of the song, its lyrics, and its theme.

5. Would the story of Jekyll and Hyde have worked just as well if Dr. Jekyll was as evil and bestial as Mr. Hyde? Discuss this.

Etymology

As interesting as the origins of a work of literature is the *etymology* of a word, the story of its genesis and evolution. If you were to look up the etymological entry in the dictionary for the word *character*, you would find:

[ME *caracter*, fr. MF *caractère*, fr. L *character* mark, distinctive quality, fr. Gk *charaktēr*, fr. *charassein* to scratch, engrave]

Translated, this means: The word *character* was derived from the Medieval English word *caracter*, also spelled *carecter*, which was derived from an earlier Greek word *charakter*, which was derived from the Greek word *charattein*, meaning, "to engrave."

From a dictionary, copy down the etymology of each of the following words, then write an explanation of what the dictionary entry means. (Your dictionary provides a list of abbreviations and symbols and what they mean.)

1. manuscript

2. dual

3. sinister

4. ornate

5. citizen

6. gallows

7. Holland

8. surgeon

9. panic

10. sadistic

Narrative Writing

The cabinet in Stevenson's boyhood home suggested/triggered the true story of Deacon Brodie in his mind. Look around your home. Then tell a true story from your life suggested by a piece of furniture, picture, knickknack, or other item. (For example, there may be an old clock given to you by someone you will always remember.)

Library and Information-Seeking Skills

1. Use a source called *DSM-IV (Diagnostic and Statistical Manual of Mental Disorders: DSM-IV)* or other resources on psychological disorders to find out about Multiple Personality Disorder. In what ways do Jekyll and Hyde fit the description?

2. Jekyll/Hyde takes a drug to change personalities. Use a book or website on the effects of drugs and alcohol to see what effects alcohol, cocaine, heroin and methamphetamines have on the personality of the user. In what ways does Hyde resemble the description of these effects?

Teacher Resources
Whole Language Activities for "A Person in Two"

Before Writing Activity

Deduction

In addition to developing the student's facility to reason deductively, the activity promotes the growth of listening and social-interaction skills, both cooperative and competitive. Moreover, it serves to pique interest in literature in general.

1. Divide the class into three or four teams. Identify them as Team 1, Team 2, Team 3, and Team 4; appoint a leader/spokesperson for each team.

2. Have students number from 1 to 20 on their papers.

3. Say: "I am going to ask 20 questions. Take notes on the questions and their answers. You will probably not know the answers right off. Instead, you will have to *deduce* them; that is, you will have to use your reasoning powers. The team that has the most correct answers will get an A; that with the second most will get a B, and so on." (Or, use any technique consistent with your own grading system.)

4. Ask the first question of Team 1. Give team members time to discuss possible answers, then have the team's spokesperson give the answer on which the group has decided. If the answer is correct, a point is scored; if incorrect, ask Team 2 the same question. Continue asking the question until it is answered correctly. Each time you ask the question of a new group, give a clue. (For example, if the answer is "2001," you may say "higher" or "lower" to each response.)

5. Continue by asking the next question of the team that numerically follows the team answering the question correctly. (For example, if Team 2 gets the right answer to the first question, then Team 3 gets first shot at the second question.)

Questions

1. What was the bestselling book for the last one hundred years in a row? (The Bible. It has been the bestselling book every year since 1500.)

2. In what year was the first paperback book published? (1841)

3. What novel by Robert Louis Stevenson was originally titled *The Sea Cook*? (*Treasure Island*)

4. Though written in English, in what European country were these first paperbacks printed? (Germany—for British and American tourists)

5. How long did it take Erle Stanley Gardner to write *The Case of the Velvet Claws*, his first mystery? (six weeks)

6. Victor Hugo, author of *Les Miserables* and other classics, ran unsuccessfully for the presidency of what country? (France)

7. At what age did Edgar Allan Poe die? (40)

8. What famous American author was the first to write a book on a typewriter? (Mark Twain/Samuel Clemens)

9. What was the name of the book he wrote? (*The Adventures of Tom Sawyer*)

10. In what year was this book written? (1875)

11. The word **mystery** comes from a Greek word meaning to do what with your eyes? (close/shut—from the Greek *myein*, meaning "to shut the eyes.")

12. Why is the ending of Charles Dickens' novel *The Mystery of Edwin Drood* a mystery that no one will ever be able to solve? (Dickens died before finishing the mystery.)

13. *Uncle Tom's Cabin*, a book depicting the evils of slavery was published in 1852 by Harriet Beecher Stowe. Ms. Stowe claimed the book was not written by her, but by whom, or what? (God)

14. Who wrote *The Joy Luck Club*? (Amy Tan)

15. What famous and presently popular magazine was first printed in the cellar of a bar in New York State? (*Reader's Digest*)

From *Great Stories Behind Famous Books*. Copyright © 1999 by Don L. Wulffson. (Alleyside Press, 1999)

16. What American President wrote *Profiles in Courage*? (Kennedy)

17. How many years did it take to write the Bible? (1,600)

18. Emily Dickinson (1830–1886) is one of America's most famous poets. How many poems did she publish during her lifetime? (Seven. She wrote in absolute secrecy and rarely shared her work, even with friends and family.)

19. To what sport was author and humorist Erma Bombeck referring when she wrote, "I never engage in a sport in which there are ambulances waiting at the bottom of the hill?" (skiing)

20. What "man-made, mechanical" word did playwright Karel Capek add to our vocabulary? (robot)

During Reading Activities

Skim Reading [Exercise sheet □]

Skim reading is an essential skill which is frequently needed on a day-to-day basis by all of us. Tell students that the following will assist them in skim reading. Focus on titles, topic sentences, proper nouns, italicized words and phrases; focus on clauses providing complete thoughts. Skip prepositions, conjunctions, definite and indefinite articles, and transitional words and phrases. Explain that the purpose of the first skim reading activity is to give them an overview of the selection; that of the second is to quickly glean required information.

After Reading Activities

Analyzing the Structure of a Piece of Writing
[Exercise sheet □]

The activity develops skill in reading carefully and in recognizing the organizational make-up of a piece of writing, especially the varied purposes of different paragraphs within a piece of writing.

Answers: (1) The second paragraph is a synopsis of the story; (2) We know that Brodie will not survive the hanging because in the third paragraph it says he "died by hanging"; (3) the next-to-last paragraph is the climax of the story of Brodie's life; (4) the last paragraph brings the selection to a close by counterpointing Brodie's life and Stevenson's literary resurrection of him.

Understanding Theme [Exercise sheet □]

The purpose of having students engage in these activities is for them to discover/recognize that they (as we all do) have both good and negative qualities. This accomplished, they begin to see how their own lives relate to the central theme of *Jekyll & Hyde*. The nature of the activities is one of active, holistic learning in which literature becomes personalized.

Etymology [Exercise sheet □]

Word origins are conceptually correlational with the origins of works of literature. The purpose of the activity is to promote students' understanding and appreciation of etymology and help them develop the necessary skills to access this information in a dictionary. An effective way to introduce students to the activity is to prepare overhead transparencies of: (1) The list of symbols and abbreviations used in their dictionary; (2) The etymological entries for various words. This will enable you to "walk students through" the job of translating the entries into understandable terms.

Narrative Writing [Exercise sheet □]

The activity is designed to do more than develop narrative writing skills. That is, it is a holistic activity which addresses a continuing motif throughout the book: that is, there is a story behind *everything*. Just as there is a story behind the writing of a book, there is a story behind an item of furniture or clothing, behind a painting or a piece of sculpture, or behind a tattoo or scar.

Library and Information-Seeking Skills
[Exercise sheet □]

1. If your library does not own *DSM-IV*, try a medical or mental health resource on Multiple Personality Disorder, or have the students use their Web browser to locate information under this search term.

2. There are a variety of reference books and websites on drugs that students may consult. In selecting a resource, encourage the students to consider those resources that were published by a major authority such as the American Medical Association or a government agency.

Chapter 3

Will You Marry Me, Alice in Wonderland?

Carroll's *Alice's Adventures in Wonderland*

One summer day in 1862 two young English scholars took three little girls on a picnic. One of the men was Charles Ludwidge Dodgson. The girls were sisters—Alice, Lorina, and Edith Liddell. During the outing, Dodgson made up a fanciful tale about a little girl who tumbled down a rabbit hole into a splendidly strange and humorous world. Because Alice was Dodgson's favorite, he called the little heroine of his story by the same name.

Alice was thrilled with the story. After hearing it, she begged Dodgson to write it down. Dodgson was a mathematics professor, not a writer. But to please Alice, that night he began writing, not stopping work until six in the morning, when he had the completed story in hand. Later, he illustrated it with his own drawings, and then presented it to little Alice Liddell as a gift. He called the story *Alice's Adventures Underground.*

Alice and her parents were enchanted with the story; among others, they showed it to Henry Kingsley, a prominent and successful novelist of the era. Kingsley told Mrs. Liddell to urge the author to seek publication. Eventually Dodgson was persuaded. But being a very shy and retiring man, he opted to hide behind a pseudonym, a pen name. By reversing his first and middle names (Charles Ludwidge), and then translating them into Latin then back to English, he arrived at "Lewis Carroll." He then polished and expanded the original manuscript, had his own drawings replaced with those of John Tenniel, a famous illustrator of the time, and changed the name of the book from *Alice's Adventures Underground* to *Alice's Adventures in Wonderland.* Published in 1865, the book was an overnight success—and eventually came to be regarded as one of the finest children's stories ever written.

Dodgson went on to write *Through the Looking Glass,* a sequel to *Alice in Wonderland.* He also wrote "The History of the Snark," the longest nonsense poem in the English language. Words and names from his fanciful writings, such as *squak, Mad Hatter,* and *Tweedledee* have become popular additions to the English language.

But what about Alice Liddell, the inspiration for the fictional Alice? What became of her? Did Dodgson, after becoming rich and famous, just forget all about her?

From here on, the story behind *Alice in Wonderland* takes a strange twist, the exact nature of which has been blurred by time. According to most literary historians, after Alice grew up, Dodgson suddenly took an intense disliking to her. She was, as he wrote in one of his letters, "someone I have no desire to ever lay eyes upon again." Why? It was rumored at the time, and it is now generally believed, that when Alice came of age, Dodgson fell desperately in love with her. He asked her to marry him. She said "thanks, but no thanks."

In 1880, Alice Liddell married a man named Reginald Hargreaves. The couple had three sons—Alan, Caryl, and Leopold. Dodgson was asked to stand as godfather to Leopold. Lending credence to the theory that Dodgson was a spurned and bitter suitor, he adamantly refused to even consider the idea.

Alan and Leopold were killed in World War I. And after her husband's death in 1926, Alice was left penniless, and without any means of supporting herself. She had only one thing she thought might be of value, Dodgson's original manuscript of *Alice's Adventures Underground.* To her astonishment, scores of critics and historians came begging for it.

Eventually she sold it to a London company for the then princely sum of $74,259. The money was a godsend. On it, Alice lived the rest of her life in ease and comfort. She died quietly, at the age of 80, in England.

Student Assignment

Fluent and Flexible Thinking

Imagine someone making up a fanciful tale about you. What sort of story would you want it to be? What would be the basic ingredients of the story so that it would be pleasing to you?

1. Would you be the main character? What would you look like? What special skills, powers, or qualities would you have?

2. What other characters/persons would be in the story with you?

3. What would be the genre of the story? For example, would it be sci-fi, horror, romance, adventure? Other?

4. Where would the story take place?

5. What are some of the things that you would like to have happen in the story?

Developing Word Skills

1. Which of the following is a homophone for the word *tale*?

   a) tail
   b) story
   c) language

2. Which of the following is an antonym for the word *fanciful*?

   a) holistic
   b) regarded
   c) realistic

3. Which of the following is *not* a synonym for the word *thrilled*?

   a) delighted
   b) ecstatic
   c) nonsense

4. Which of these words is onomatopoeic?

   a) squawk
   b) popular
   c) poverty-stricken.

   (Give an example of at least one more onomatopoeic word.)

5. Which of the following is a well-known pseudonym?

   a) mathematics
   b) Dodgson
   c) Mark Twain.

   (Give an example of at least one more pseudonym.)

6. Which of the following is euphemistic?

   a) died
   b) bit the dust
   c) passed away.

   (Give an example of at least one more euphemism.)

7. Which of the following words (from the same

From *Great Stories Behind Famous Books.* Copyright © 1999 by Don L. Wulffson. (Alleyside Press, 1999)

line of poetry) is a neologism?

a) he
b) went
c) galumphing
d) back

Pre-Reading Inventory

Answer these questions to the best of your ability before reading the selection.

1. In what century was *Alice in Wonderland* written?

2. What subject did the author of this work teach in school?

3. What all-important feature did John Tenniel add to the book?

4. In what country was *Alice in Wonderland* written and first published?

5. Who wrote *Alice in Wonderland*?

6. What was the original title of *Alice in Wonderland*?

Inferential Thinking

Complete each statement with a logical inference.

1. If Alice had not begged Dodgson to write down the story, _____

   _____

2. If the story had been told using Lorina as the heroine, _____

   _____

3. If Dodgson had been an English professor rather than a mathematics professor,

   _____

   _____

4. The name Lewis Carroll is far better known than Charles Dodgson because _____

   _____

5. Lewis Carroll probably had his illustrations replaced with ones done by John Tenniel

because _____

   _____

6. Today, the original manuscript of *Alice's Adventures Underground* _____

   _____

7. If Dodgson and Alice had married,

   _____

   _____

Oral Inflection

A: Read each of the following sentences aloud, emphasizing the word in **bold italics**.

1. From here on, the story of *Alice in Wonderland* takes **several** twists, some sad, some strange.

2. From here on the story of *Alice in Wonderland* takes several twists, some sad, some **strange**.

3. **This** piece of rudeness was more than Alice could bear.

4. This piece of **rudeness** was more than Alice could bear.

5. This piece of rudeness was **more** than Alice could bear.

6. This piece of rudeness was more than **Alice** could bear.

7. "Really, **now** you ask me," said Alice.

8. "Really, now **you** ask me," said Alice.

9. "Really, now you ask **me**," said Alice.

B: Briefly explain the difference between sentences 7, 8, and 9. What effects do the differences of inflection make? What slight—but notable—differences are there in terms of meaning?

Writing with Personification

Complete each sentence in such a way that the object has human qualities.

   Example: The trees *bowed to the wind, their shaggy, green heads almost touching the ground.*

From *Great Stories Behind Famous Books*. Copyright © 1999 by Don L. Wulffson. (Alleyside Press, 1999)

1. The mountain _____.

2. The incoming tide _____.

3. The iceberg _____.

4. The clock on the wall _____.

5. The clouds _____.

Fanciful Writing

What would it be like if a shoe could talk? Or how about a chair? Or maybe a pencil? Here is a humorous and unusual play in which a person ("Me") is talking to a football.

Me and My Football

(I'm sitting in the park, talking to my football.)

Me: How's it going today, Football?

Football: Lousy!

Me: How come?

Football: 'Cause I'm sick of being kicked around by you.

Me: Sorry, but you were invented for that.

Football: I'm not too thrilled about being tossed around, either.
It makes me dizzy. Especially when I'm thrown in a spiral.

Me: That's how you have to be tossed—due to your weird shape.

Football: Oh yeah, now start making fun of my figure!

Me: Look, I'm not making fun of your figure!

Football: Yes, you are. And another thing…

Me: Oh, be quiet.

(Just then a bunch of my friends show up. I give my football a good kick and send it flying in their direction.)

Write your own play in which you are talking to an object of your choice. From beginning to end, use the structure of the above play.

Library and Information-Seeking Skills

1. Find the real names of three other authors who use pen names or pseudonyms. Did you find any authors who use multiple pen names? If possible, find out the story behind one of those pen names—how was it chosen?

2. Use a dictionary to find the origins and definitions of the word pseudonym.

3. One of Dodgson's contemporaries was his illustrator, John Tenniel. Using print resources and the Internet, find two or three interesting facts about John Tenniel.

4. What was the Victorian attitude toward invention? How is it reflected in Dodgson's book? Try the following URL or other websites on Victorian times or on Lewis Carroll:

   www.stg.brown.deu/projects/hypertext/landow/victorian/carroll/ansay.html

   Select "Inventions in *Alice in Wonderland.*"

Teacher Resources
Whole Language Activities for
"Will You Marry Me, Alice in Wonderland?"

Before Reading Activities

Fluent and Flexible Thinking [Exercise sheet ☐]
After students have written their answers, collect the papers. Say: "Your answers possibly reveal more about you than you realize. For example, they indicate: (1) Your reading preferences; (2) The kind of person you would like to be; (3) The kinds of things you like to do, et cetera." Without giving names, read some of the answers aloud. Ask the class what the answers suggest or reveal about the person.

Developing Word Skills [Exercise sheet ☐]
The purpose of the activity is to develop dictionary skills and to acquaint (and reacquaint) students with terms commonly used in language arts. Ensuring this relationship will prove useful during discussions and in correcting student work.
Answers: (1) a, (2) c, (3) c, (4) a, (5) c , (6) c, (7) c.

Pre-Reading Inventory [Exercise sheet ☐]
This item gives both the teacher and the students an idea of their familiarity with the contents of the selection.

During Reading Activities

1. Have students skim read the selection to correct their answers to the "pre-reading inventory."

2. Read the story aloud with the class. Alternate between paragraphs with students. That is, after reading every other paragraph, call on a student to read that which follows.

After Reading Activities

Inferential Thinking [Exercise sheet ☐]
Before students begin work, explain the difference between information that is *stated* and that which is *inferred*, derived through reasoning. For example, it is stated that Dodgson used the pseudonym Lewis

Carroll. We can infer from the way he derived the pen name that he was a highly educated man who entertained himself with scholarly and somewhat arcane thoughts.

Oral Inflection [Exercise sheet ☐]
Students will discover how altering oral emphasis can change the meaning of a sentence—read aloud, subvocally, or silently.

1. Read the first two items to the class. Then have a student read 3 through 6 aloud, and another read 7 through 9.

2. Discuss the questions with students.

3. Call on students to read sentences from the selection using the oral emphasis they feel appropriate.

Writing with Personification [Exercise sheet ☐]

1. Collect the papers and read aloud the different responses to each item.

2. As homework, assign the reading of a story which contains a significant amount of figurative language. Have students find examples of personification, as well as simile and metaphor.

Creative/Fanciful Writing [Exercise sheet ☐]
It is highly important that students not only write creatively but also think creatively. The message to them (whether tacit or explicit) is that *they*, like the writers they are reading about, have their own creative proclivities and talents, and the ability to think imaginatively.

1. Make a transparency of "Me and My Football." Read the narrative portion as two students return the dialogue.

2. Before students begin to write, review the structure of the play. Also, brainstorm with students by asking for objects that might be used in their play, and write these on the board.

3. When students have finished, make three photocopies of some of the better plays. Have students read these aloud (with one reading the narrative and the other two reading the dialogue).

Library and Information-Seeking Skills

[Exercise sheet ☐]

1. This question can be used to demonstrate how the library catalog and other indexes cross reference author pseudonyms.

2. Recommend that students compare the information they find in an abridged dictionary with an unabridged dictionary.

3. This question will require access to more extensive biographical resources such as *Who Was Who* or an art encyclopedia. However, some information on the illustrator can also be located on the Web using the illustrator's name.

4. If the recommended website is inactive, suggest that the students use the Boolean search features of their Internet browser by combining several terms such as *Victorian Era* AND *invention*.

Chapter 4

Vlad Tepes The Real Dracula

Stoker's *Dracula*

It is disturbing yet true. It is hard to explain, but vampire legends have been around since the beginning of recorded history, and the legends existed independently in almost every culture on earth. Why? The answer is unsettling. It may be one you do not want to hear. But perhaps the reason they have been around so long and in so many places is that there really are vampires.

The legends and stories are part of the folklore of the people of Africa, Europe, Asia, and parts of the Middle East. The legends are strikingly similar. Always, the vampires are people who have turned into the living dead. By day, they sleep in a supine position in coffins, crypts and graves. By night, to continue their gruesome existence, and to renew their vitality, they must drink the blood of human victims. Usually, a vampire can be killed only by a stake driven through its heart; then its head must be chopped off and its body burned.

1)_____?_____. Old superstitions said that people who committed suicide turned into vampires. So did—according to the legends—the seventh son of a seventh son, those born with teeth, and those bitten by vampires. Such ideas have been taken *very* seriously. For example, in 1823 in England a law had to be passed to deter people from the practice of driving stakes through the hearts of those who had committed suicide!

In the 1890s Irishman Bram Stoker decided to write a novel about a vampire. The legends and lore of vampirism had always fascinated him, and he had studied them for years. At first Stoker was going to use a make-believe character as the protagonist. Then one day a friend of his told him about Vlad Tepes.

"I don't know if Tepes was actually a vampire," Stoker's friend told him. "But this man was so vicious and bloodthirsty it's utterly terrifying!"

2) _____?_____. Tepes, he found, lived during the fifteenth century in a dark, forbidding castle in Transylvania. The man was a sadist; his hobby, if it can be described so innocuously, was torturing people. He skinned people, cut them into pieces, or buried them alive. But his favorite method of killing was impalement. Starting from the bottom of the torso, he and his bloody henchmen slowly rammed a sharpened stake upward through the victim's body. Then the stake was fixed upright in the ground where the victim would die, writhing in incredible agony. Sometimes Tepes had hundreds of people impaled at a time, then enjoyed dining outdoors, among them. When one of his own soldiers complained about the awful stench of rotting bodies, Tepes immediately had the man impaled—but on a higher stake, so he would not have to smell the others!

3)_____?_____. One day a group of Turkish ambassadors came to greet the prince officially. He ordered them to take off their turbans. They refused, explaining that it was their custom to keep them on at all times. "Then you will wear them forever!" screamed Tepes. As his guards held down the screaming ambassadors, Tepes nailed the turbans to their heads!

The people of the time had a nickname for Vlad Tepes. This nickname, meaning "son of the devil," was Dracula. And that is the name Stoker used in his book, and a name which is now known worldwide.

Stoker's novel *Dracula,* published in 1897, was an overnight success. In the novel, an Englishman visits Count Dracula, only to find himself a prisoner in the count's castle. As the plot evolves, an ongoing battle ensues between the Englishman's band of vampire hunters and Dracula with his morbid but loyal gypsy servants.

In 1922 a movie was made that was based on Stoker's book; it was a silent film called *Nosferatu.* In 1931 came a more famous film, *Dracula,* which starred Bela Lugosi. Since then there have been dozens more Dracula films, some serious, some rather campy and comedic.

As for the real Dracula, Vlad Tepes, you may wonder what became of him. He was killed in a battle with the Turks. He was decapitated and his head was sent to the Sultan of Turkey in Constantinople. In a fitting end for Dracula, his head was impaled on a stake, then put on exhibit and left to rot.

After Bram Stoker made Dracula a household word, other writers and producers began concocting stories about female vampires. The inspiration for them, as with the male vampires, was a real-life monster.

Her name was Elizabeth Bathory (1560–1614), the Countess of Nadasy, a province in ancient Hungary. The countess did not drink blood, she *bathed* in it! One after the other, she employed naive, young girls as servants. But not to dust and tidy up her castle. She wanted their blood! Paranoically terrified of growing old, the countess believed that she would stay young and live forever by taking beauty baths in an iron tub filled with the blood of young girls. Sometimes her male servants butchered the girls on the spot and filled the tub to the brim with their blood. Other girls were imprisoned, kept barely alive, and every so often had some of their blood drained into a bucket. Gleefully, the insane countess then smeared her hands and face with blood and gore.

Finally, after she had killed more than 50 girls, Elizabeth was found out. Her servants were executed, and she was imprisoned in a room in her castle. Turning old and gray, there she stayed until her dying day.

Student Assignment

Writing Analysis: The Topic Sentence

A topic sentence introduces the contents of the paragraph as a whole. Three topic sentences, which are given below, are missing from the selection "Vlad Tepes: The Real Dracula." Skim the selection and, on your own paper, determine where the topic sentences belong.

a. Stoker read every book he could find about Vlad Tepes.

b. There have been many explanations for vampirism.

c. There is another especially horrid story about Tepes.

Personal Response to What You Read

As you read the selection silently, write down:

1. One item you find especially unpleasant and disturbing.

2. One bit of information you find especially interesting and informative.

Writing with Understatement

A: Complete the following.

Example: Being impaled alive might hurt a little.

1. Vlad Tepes was a man who

_____

2. As to the number of vampire movies, you might say

_____

3. When I saw the corpse move its hand, I

_____

B: Write four understatements. The first is about a hot day, the second about an accident of some kind, the third about failing a test, and the last about anything of your own choosing.

1.

2.

3.

4.

The Sentence Structure of Questions

Questions can begin with interrogatives (words such as who, what, where, when, why, how). They can also be created by inverting the sentence structure so that the verb comes before the subject.

> ***Example:*** *The answer IS creepy. IS the answer creepy?*

Change each of the following into questions by altering the sentence structure. (Do not omit any of the information contained in any of the sentences.)

1. The legends are strikingly similar.

2. Stoker's novel *Dracula*, published in 1897, was an overnight success.

3. Her servants were executed, and she was imprisoned in a room in her castle.

4. In 1922 a movie was made that was based on Stoker's book; it was a silent film called *Nosferatu.*

5. At first Stoker was going to use a make-believe character as the protagonist.

Writing: Paragraphs and Topic Sentences

A: Sequencing The following paragraph is in the wrong order. Study it, then rewrite it with the sentences in the correct order.

a. He later shipped out as a sailor on a slave ship, where he flogged one man to death and murdered another.

b. After the war he became a pirate and dealer in slaves.

c. John Paul Jones is an individual whose reputation is greater than the man himself. He ended his career as a commodore in the Russian navy.

d. Fleeing to America, he assumed the name Jones to avoid detection, eventually distinguishing himself during the American revolution.

e. Born in Scotland and originally named John Paul, he became an actor at the age of eleven.

B: Write a paragraph which summarizes the contents of "Vlad Tepes: The Real Dracula," being sure to use an appropriate topic sentence.

Library and Information-Seeking Skills

1. What other authors have used the legends and tales surrounding vampires to create their own vampire stories? Create a bibliography of ten or more books and stories, giving author, title and year of publication.

2. Bela Lugosi was an actor famous for his role as Dracula. Using the American Film Institute website or another film source, make a filmography (list of films) about vampires, including some of Lugosi's films. Your filmography should include film title, year released, and name of main actor/actress.

3. Other types of monsters, creatures or legends have been made famous in books and movies. Name two other types of monsters, creatures, legends, or myths, and list five or more books or stories about them. Using the same sources as in the question 2, create a filmography for films about one of these creatures.

From *Great Stories Behind Famous Books.* Copyright © 1999 by Don L. Wulffson. (Alleyside Press, 1999)

Teacher Resources
Whole Language Activities for
"Vlad Tepes: The Real Dracula"

Before Reading Activities

Scrambles Word Warm-Up

The goals of this activity are:

* Promoting the development of speaking and social-interaction skills, both cooperative and competitive

* Development of spelling and vocabulary skills

* Preparing the student for words that will be encountered in the selection

* Arousing enthusiasm for the reading selection, and promoting a positive attitude toward learning in general. The activity is fun, "kid-friendly," and creates an active, pleasant classroom atmosphere.

Directions:

1. Divide the class into two teams.

2. Say: "Using an overhead projector, I will be putting scrambled words on the screen." (The words come from the reading selection that follows, "Vlad Tepes: The Real Dracula")

3. Say: "I will put the scrambled words on the screen one at a time. As soon as you think you know the word, call it out. A correct answer scores one point for your team. When a correct answer is given, I will then call on another member of your team to spell the word. As that person spells the word, I will write down as much of the word as is spelled correctly, stopping when an incorrect letter is given."

4. Say: "The following is an example." Show the scrambled word: U T N B A R. Say: "The answer is TURBAN. If the class were to have difficulty in identifying the word, I might give a clue such as 'headgear.' If someone were to start spelling the word TUA, I would write down only the correct part of the response, T U, and then call on a member of the *opposite* team to spell the remain-der of the word, going back and forth from team to team until the entire word is spelled correctly. The team whose member finishes the word correctly scores a point."

5. Say: "Everyone on the winning team in the contest gets an A, everyone on the other team a C" (or use any formula compatible with your grading system).

Optional Procedure: Divide the class into several teams, appointing a leader for each. Have teams work on paper in unscrambling the words, giving grades as per those who finish first, second, etc.

The Words:

1. P A V I E M (vampire)
2. N A Y G O N (agony)
3. E D L E G N (legend)
4. O T R O S (torso)
5. R I P C E N (prince)
6. R R T T U O E (torture)
7. L O V E V E (evolve)
8. D A B A S A R M S O (ambassador)
9. I X H B T E I (exhibit)
10. A N T I P S R O G O T (protagonist)
11. U E N S E (ensue)
12. M E C H N N H E (henchmen)
13. T R Y C P (crypt)
14. E D R T E (deter)
15. G N O O G N I (ongoing)

Note: Give clues. If you wish, give more words.

The activity tends to be one that kids enjoy and that gets the class period off to a fast, enthusiastic beginning. If you wish, use the activity to inaugurate other reading selections.

From *Great Stories Behind Famous Books.* Copyright © 1999 by Don L. Wulffson. (Alleyside Press, 1999)

Optional Assignments

1. As classwork or homework, have the students write each word in an original sentence and/or write a definition.

2. Give a vocabulary test on the words.

Writing Analysis: Topic Sentence [Exercise sheet □]

Say: "A topic sentence introduces the contents of the paragraph as a whole. Three topic sentences, which are given below, are missing from the selection "Vlad Tepes: The Real Dracula". Skim read the selection and, on your own paper, determine where the topic sentences belong."

a. Stoker read every book he could find about Vlad Tepes. (2)

b. There have been many explanations for vampirism. (1)

c. There is another especially horrid story about Tepes. (3)

During Reading Activities

Personal (Affective & Cognitive) Response

[Exercise sheet □]

A. Call on students to read aloud the paragraphs that were missing a topic sentence.

B. Have students read the selection silently. As they do, have them write down:

   1. One item they find especially unpleasant and disturbing;

   2. One bit of information they find especially interesting and informative.

After Reading Activities

Personal (Affective & Cognitive) Response

Discuss with the students their responses to the second "During Reading Activities." As to their affective response to an item in the selection they found disturbing, ask them to look within themselves as to why it bothered them. *Example:* "I identified with the person's pain." Or: "In today's world, similarly cruel acts are committed."

As to their cognitive response to the item they found especially interesting, ask them: "Why was some information more interesting to you than other infor-mation?" Also, ask: "Why do we often find it pleasurable to learn?"

Dracula in Film

Show a movie or video of one of the early Dracula films. *Nosferatu* or the original *Dracula* would be especially intriguing for young people to see.

Writing with Understatement [Exercise sheet □]

The goal of the activity is for students to recognize understatement (spoken or written) and to employ this linguistic device, both in their writing and speaking. Point out to students that understatement can be used for sarcastic and/or humorous effect.

The Sentence Structure of Questions

[Exercise sheet □]

It would be helpful in presenting this lesson to create an overhead transparency. To the degree you find necessary, work with the students in completing the activity.

Writing: Paragraphs and Topic Sentence

[Exercise sheet □]

A. To whatever degree you find necessary, assist students with the activity by helping them locate the topic sentence. [Answers: (a) 3; (b) 1; (c) 5; (d) 4; (e) 2.] After they have finished, show them how the paragraph can be written with the topic sentence at the end of the paragraph. Use the following (understated/snide) topic sentence:

   You might say that John Paul Jones is an individual whose reputation is a bit greater than the man himself.

B. Suggest that students try writing their synoptic paragraph with the topic sentence at the end.

Library and Information-Seeking Skills

[Exercise sheet □]

1. *The Readers' Advisor* is a good source of information, but the Web can also be searched using any major browser.

2. The URL for the American Film Institute is: www.afionline.org

3. The print or electronic version of *The Readers' Guide to Periodical Literature* can be searched to identify other monsters.

From *Great Stories Behind Famous Books.* Copyright © 1999 by Don L. Wulffson. (Alleyside Press, 1999)

Chapter 5

The Genius
The Lives of the Brontes

The time: The early nineteenth century. The place: A joyless, dismal-looking house in northern England. Its stone walls are dark, cold, and seem to weep the wetness that permeates the dreary countryside. The family: A minister, a stern and pious man; three daughters—Charlotte, Anne, and Emily Jane; and just one son, Branwell.

Branwell was the center of that small universe. In those times, boys were considered superior to girls. In addition, Branwell was handsome, robust, suave—and he was gifted. A genius, in fact. At an early age, he demonstrated remarkable artistic and literary talents. His sketches and paintings, his poetry and prose—all, it seemed, presaged a brilliant future for the young man.

All the family's hopes rested on the boy. His parents doted on him, and sacrificed for him. As did his sisters. Females, it was their job to wait upon their talented brother, serve him, cater to his needs—and his budding genius. And make do as best they could for themselves. Quietly, ungrudgingly, it was expected that they sacrifice, do without—to whatever degree necessary—so that Branwell would realize his full potential.

When he came of age, it was decided that Branwell should attend college. The girls crimped and saved, worked as governesses and servants, earning extra money so that their brother could receive a proper education. While the girls were tutored at home in the basics by an aunt, Branwell, with money earned by his sisters, was sent to London to study at the Royal Academy of the Arts.

He saw little of the inside of the college; he rarely attended classes. Though repeatedly admon-ished, he showed no contrition, and no inclination to change his ways. He failed every subject, and was asked to leave. A few weeks after his promising departure for school, he returned home—wholly uneducated—except in the arts of drinking, gambling, and chasing women. His pockets were empty; the money his parents and sisters had worked so long and hard to save for him had all been squandered.

Still, the family's hopes for Branwell remained undiminished. His genius, his father concluded, had simply been misunderstood. In fact, it was not really Branwell who had failed at college; rather, it was the college which had failed the boy—proving itself inadequate to properly instruct, guide, and shape the talents of one whose genius was undoubtedly beyond their own.

Work. That was what Branwell needed, his father decided. As a student, he had been wasting his time. He was too good for that, too advanced, both intellectually and artistically. No, instead of a student, the young man should be a teacher. And as a teacher, there would be sufficient time for him to paint and write, and otherwise develop his own many and varied talents.

The family—the father and the three sisters—were unable to secure Branwell a regular teaching job; however, they did find him a position as a private tutor.

Once again, Branwell made a premature return home. He had been fired; he had made no money, but instead had frittered away every cent his family had given him. Excuses. Other than with a long list of excuses, he returned home empty-handed.

As his failures continued to pile up, so did Branwell's excuses—all of them flimsy and bogus, all of them lies. The truth: With each passing year, the young man was slipping more and more into a directionless, unmotivated life of dissipation and self-indulgence. Art and scholarship—they no longer held his interest; rather, it was loose women, carousing, gambling, alcohol, and opium which had become the substance and subject matter of his day-to-day existence. The once vital, robust young man was now a frail, sickly vestige of his former self.

Though fully aware of this, his sisters did not lose faith in him. He would turn his life around, they were sure, and they continued to believe that he would one day succeed, be universally acclaimed for the highly gifted—albeit somewhat disturbed genius—they knew him to be.

They continued to support him. They scrimped; they cut corners on household expenses; they did without; they hired themselves out at whatever work they could find, most often as governesses and maids.

All to no avail.

Today, almost two hundred years later, no one studies—or even cares to look upon—Branwell's paintings. No one reviews—or bothers to read—his dull, vapid writings.

In 1848, Branwell died of tuberculosis. His passing was met by the public not with weeping but with smirks. An unmitigated failure, in the public eye he was a pathetic figure, and was openly ridiculed and mocked.

During the years of Branwell's dissipation and unproductive dabblings in writing, his three sisters had put the time to good use. Modestly, quietly—without fanfare or presumption—they had applied themselves to one of the endeavors at which their brother had failed so dismally—writing. Perhaps to relieve the dullness and drudgery of their own harsh, narrow lives—in their spare time, usually late at night by candlelight—they attempted to pursue the literary prominence they had for so long assumed was their brother's birthright, his destiny.

He did not succeed—at all.

But *they* did—in every conceivable way.

For the three sisters who gave Branwell their unflagging devotion and unwavering confidence, and who unselfishly subsidized his useless life, are persons whose works you will immediately recognize:

Anne authored the novel *Agnes Grey*.

Emily wrote the classic *Wuthering Heights*.

And Charlotte penned the immortal *Jane Eyre*.

Anne, Emily, and Charlotte … Bronte.

All three works were tremendously successful. All three were published within a year. And all three, as you know, were written by sisters. Such a feat had never before been accomplished; in all probability, it will never be achieved again.

A last, final touch to an already ironic story. In their day and age, the public generally frowned upon women even attempting to write. It was believed that writing was the domain of males; this complex, sophisticated, highly cerebral art form was one which only men were considered competent to undertake, Thus, when the sisters' works were published it was under the pseudonyms of Ellis, Currer, and Acton Bell. Men—in order to sell their works—the three women had disguised themselves as being of the same gender as Branwell, their unsuccessful brother.

From *Great Stories Behind Famous Books*. Copyright © 1999 by Don L. Wulffson. (Alleyside Press, 1999)

Student Assignment

Discussion and Debate

1. For the first 1,700 years of this century, there were almost no female writers of any note. Why do you believe this is the case?

2. Debate. This may be a one-on-one debate, or a "panel" debate.

   Consider one or more (or all) of these questions:

   a) Men are primarily the reason women have been oppressed and have, in many areas, failed to achieve as much as men.

   b) Women are not as strong as men.

   c) There are more similarities between men and women than there are differences.

   d) Men do not like strong women.

   e) Both men and women are struggling at present to define their roles in society.

Dictionary Skills: Pronunciation

Following each word in the dictionary is its pronunciation. A pronunciation guide (or key) can be found at the front of the dictionary which provides an explanation of the various symbols. For each of the following phonetic/symbolic pronunciations, locate the word in the selection and write it down. Secondly, define the word, giving the dictionary definition appropriate to the word as used in the context of the selection.

1. \'dis -ə -pā - shən\

2. \'pī - əs\

3. \sə -'rē - brəl\

4. \pə -'ten- shəl\

5. \'ves - tij\

6. \'kän - trīt\

7. \'səb-sə-dīz\

8. \swäv\

9. \òl-'bē -it\

10. \'vap - əd\

Critical Thinking

1. Is it possible that the great expectations for Branwell contributed to his downfall? Discuss.

2. All three of the sisters' novels are, to varying degrees, romances, and the protagonists in each case are morally strong, resolute young women. Discuss these facts in light of the lives the Bronte sisters lived.

3. In 1847, a critic by the name of James Lorimer reviewed *Wuthering Heights*. He wrote: "Here are all the faults of *Jane Eyre* (by Charlotte Bronte) magnified a thousandfold, and the only consolation which we have in reflecting upon it is that it will never be generally read." Write a brief review of Mr. Lorimer's review.

4. When *Wuthering Heights*, *Agnes Grey*, and *Jane Eyre* first appeared, there was considerable conjecture that all three works had been written by the same person. What reasons could have led to this conclusion?

5. Charlotte's first novel, *The Professor*, was rejected repeatedly, and was not published until after her death. What did *Jane Eyre*, in your opinion, have to do with the posthumous publication of this work?

6. The history of the Bronte family has stirred more interest than that of the families of most writers. In your opinion, what is the reason for this?

7. Do modern women writers owe a debt of gratitude to the Bronte sisters? Explain.

Comparative and Analytical Thinking

The following was written by a well-known, modern writer, Martha Grimes. As you read it carefully, jot down reasons why it could not possibly have been written by one of the Bronte sisters.

Diane Demorney, purveyor of arcane bits of information, adjusted the cigarette in her mouth as a signal for someone to light it. As she leaned forward, her hair, black as a buzzard, formed a razor-sharp wing across her cheekbone. Diane was good-looking in a rapacious, raptorlike way. She kept her fashion-model body all planes and angles; her lipstick was blood red; her nails as sharp as tiny scythes. (From *Rainbow's End* by Martha Grimes. Ballantine Books, 1995.)

Writing

Choose one of the following:

A. Write a story containing the following elements, setting it in any locale or time-period of your choice. A young woman, her clothes old-fashioned and her hair in a bun, lives alone on a ranch that is defunct-looking yet well-provisioned, orderly, and tastefully decorated. There are two freshly dug and filled-in pits behind the place. She has just finished burying something behind the ranch house early one evening when a man appears. His clothes are shabby, yet he is wearing new-looking, patent-leather shoes. A deep scar runs from the outer corner of his left eye to his chin.

B. Write a paper in which you compare and contrast the lives of one of the Bronte sisters and any female author of your choosing.

Library and Information-Seeking Skills

1. What was the role of opium in history? Write a paragraph about opium, its use, effects, and current status. Is opium illegal now? Was it illegal in the past? Was Branwell unusual in becoming an opium user in his time period?

2. Check two or three standard sources on British literature. What do they have to say about Branwell Bronte? In comparison, what do they have to say about Charlotte, Emily, and Anne Bronte? Try the website:

    www.lang.nagoya-u.ac.jp/~matsuoka/Bronte.html

    (The Bronte Sisters Web) or search the Internet for other websites.

3. The Bronte sisters' works were published originally under men's names in order to be more successful. Use a source on women's literature to find the name of another woman author from the eighteenth or nineteenth centuries whose work is now recognized. Did that author encounter any difficulties or prejudice in being an author during that time period?

4. Find a synopsis of the plots of the three books by the Bronte sisters. List any similarities and differences in the three plots.

Teacher Resources
Whole Language Activities for "The Genius"

Before Reading Activity

Discussion and Debate [Exercise sheet ☐]

The purpose of this activity is to teach students to consider the primary motif of the selection and to see it in a contemporary light. Additional goals are to develop critical thinking and speaking skills. The first item is intended as a warm-up activity for the debate. One debate team may consist entirely of females, the other of males; or, students may take opposing views regardless of gender. The teacher should moderate the debate, requiring that students speak only one at a time.

During Reading Activity

1. Have the students read the selection silently.

2. Have a male and a female student read it aloud, alternating paragraphs.

After Reading Activities

Dictionary Skills: Pronunciation
[Exercise sheet ☐]

The purpose of the activity is to familiarize students with an essential and highly useful dictionary skill; that is, using guides to pronunciation. Make an overhead transparency of the dictionary's key to pronunciation, containing its symbols and diacritical marks. A transparency should also be made of the pronunciation guide following each of the first few words. Work aloud with the students as they undertake this activity.

Answers:

(1) dissipation, (2) pious, (3) cerebral, (4) potential, (5) vestige, (6) contrite, (7) subsidize, (8) suave, (9) albeit, (10) vapid.

Critical and Analytical Thinking Sections
[Exercise sheet ☐]

The purpose of these items is to encourage students to think critically and to develop speaking and writing skills. Moreover, it encourages them to look in depth at an author in relation to his or her times, background, and personal circumstances. Finally, it asks of them to see a literary work in relation to other literature.

Writing [Exercise sheet ☐]

The first choice fosters creative writing skills. Both choices further augment the Whole Language approach to language-arts development. That is, the "whole child" is engaged in the complex interactive growth of speaking, reading, listening, and writing skills.

Library and Information-Seeking Skills
[Exercise sheet ☐]

1. The goal of this exercise is to give the students insight into the different sources of information on opium. Encourage them to use periodical indexes, reference books, and CD-ROM resources, and to compare the depth of information each resource can offer.

2. If the library does not have any reference books containing information on Branwell Bronte, use this as an opportunity to encourage the students to ask the reference librarian about cooperative reference service agreements with larger libraries. Explain that many smaller libraries have agreements with larger systems to provide "back-up" reference service.

3. *The Readers' Advisor* is a good source of information on this subject.

4. *Masterplots* is a common resource found in many libraries.

Chapter 6

The Birth of Frankenstein

Shelley's Frankenstein

Frankenstein is one of the most widely known and most chilling tales of horror ever written. In this novel, a young student by the name of Victor Frankenstein creates a soulless monster out of parts of corpses stolen from graveyards and dissecting rooms. Frankenstein imbues his creature with life through the use of electricity.

Almost as disturbing and unusual as the book is the story behind its writing. One might imagine its author to have been a fearsome man with a dark, morose disposition and a lifelong fascination with the macabre. But this was not the case at all; this masterful work of horror was written by a very pretty and demure young woman. Her name was Mary Shelley, and she penned *Frankenstein* when she was only twenty years old.

Mary came from a rich literary background. Her father, William Godwin, was one of the most noted English authors of the time. Mary's mother was also a writer. Her book *A Vindication of the Rights of Woman* was one of the first published works to promote the doctrine of gender equality. Young Mary soon began following in her parents' footsteps, quietly filling notebook after notebook with her own stories and fantasies.

In 1814, when Mary was seventeen, a man entered her life, changing it forever. He was Percy Bysshe Shelley. One of England's most renowned poets, Shelley would lead Mary to write *Frankenstein*; and he would also fill her life with scandal and relentless, seemingly endless tragedy.

Percy Shelley was married when he first met Mary. However, he soon fell hopelessly in love with her—and she with him. In the summer of 1814, the two ran off to France together, and later married. Broken-hearted, near insane with distress, Shelley's wife committed suicide by drowning herself. That was the first tragedy. More disaster lurked. Before she was twenty, Mary had given birth to three children. Before she was twenty-two, all three had died.

During these painful and tumultuous years, Mary began writing in earnest. Percy Shelley believed she had great talent and encouraged her constantly and with unbridled enthusiasm. In 1817 she published her first book, *History of a Six Week's Tour*. By the time of its publication, she had already begun a novel, which was entitled *Hate*.

Before the completion of this book, Percy, Mary, and Mary's half sister Claire traveled to Geneva, Switzerland. There, they met the famous poet Lord Byron and an eccentric doctor by the name of Polidori. At night the group would get together and talk for hours.

During one of these late-night conversations, the subject turned to ghost stories. Lord Byron suggested a competition. All five would write a "tale of horror"; and after completion of his or her work, each would read it aloud for the others, and a winner would be selected.

Day after day, Mary struggled to think of a story. In her diary she wrote that "with every fiber of [her] being" she desired to contrive a tale that would make the reader " … dread to look round, to curdle the blood, and quicken the beating of the heart." But nothing would come to mind. The other members of the group had already begun their stories; Mary, deeply distressed with herself, was unable to even make a start.

From *Great Stories Behind Famous Books*. Copyright © 1999 by Don L. Wulffson. (Alleyside Press, 1999)

Then one night the story came to her—in a dream, a strange vision. She saw a " … pale student kneeling beside a man he had put together," a creature made of the parts of dead bodies.

Mary wrote a short story based on her dream. She won the contest—with no competition, since none of the others had finished their tales. Later, Mary expanded the story into a novel—*Frankenstein - or the Modern Prometheus*, which was published in 1818—under her own—female—name, in defiance of the conventions of the times. Critics and the reading public were fascinated with the work, not only because the story line was unique and terrifying, but because its theme plumbed a grave concern of the nineteenth and twentieth centuries: the potentially disastrous consequences of science, of people meddling with the natural order of things. The book became an instant bestseller.

Mary was not able to enjoy her success for long. In 1822, her husband, Percy, went sailing with two friends off the coast of Italy. A squall arose, the boat overturned, and all on board drowned.

This was the final—and most devastating—tragedy of Mary's life. After Percy's death, she continued to write. She produced four novels, five biographies, and many short stories. But she was an empty, emotionally destitute human being. She had lost her children and her husband. Even fame eluded her. She was a female author in a day when, as you know, writing was thought to be something only men should do; for this reason, public and critical acclaim were denied her. The name *Frankenstein* is known the world over. The name Mary Shelley is known only to those with a healthy knowledge and understanding of literary history.

Student Assignment

Comparative and Introspective Thinking

A: Put a 5, 4, 3, 2, or 1 next to each item in terms of how much it frightens you, with 5 representing the most frightening phrase.

1. An invasion by creatures from another planet.

2. The spread of a deadly new virus capable of killing everyone on earth.

3. Breaking your arm.

4. Finding out that someone you love is dying.

5. A worldwide nuclear war in which you are one of the few survivors.

6. A person made of the parts of dead people.

7. Failing a class.

8. A drought.

9. Having cavities filled at the dentist.

10. Hearing about a terrible plane crash.

11. Seeing a horror movie.

12. Witnessing someone being hit by a car.

13. A comet striking the Earth.

B: For each item, explain why it frightens you to the degree it does.

C: There is an important difference between items 9 and 10, and between 11 and 12. Compare each pair of items.

Science Fiction

1. Which items on the list would you consider to be *futuristic*? That is, which are predictions which belong in the realm of science fiction?

2. In your opinion, to what extent does science fiction depend upon guessing what the future may hold?

3. Is science fiction, in your opinion, usually about things we fear? If so, to what extent are these fears legitimate?

4. Many people enjoy books, movies, and plays that are frightening. Are you such a person? Whether you are or are not, why do you think people seek to be frightened by these media?

5. Can anything important and/or useful be learned from science fiction?

Vocabulary Development

A: The context of a sentence in which you find a word can help determine its meaning. After reading each sentence, decide what you think each **bold italicized** word(s) means and write down your answer.

1. Percy Shelley was one of England's most **renowned** poets.

2. This masterful work of horror was written by a very pretty, **demure**, and modest young woman.

3. A **squall** arose, the boat was overturned, and all on board were drowned.

4. During these painful and **tumultuous** years, Mary began writing in earnest.

5. Dr. Frankenstein **imbues** his creature with life through the use of electricity.

6. The book **plumbs** a grave concern of the nineteenth and twentieth centuries.

7. Mary published her novel under her own—female—name, in **defiance** of the **conventions** of the times.

8. One might imagine its author to have been a fearsome man with a dark, **morose** disposition and a lifelong fascination with the **macabre**.

B: Now, compare your answers with those in the dictionary. Keep in mind the dictionary often gives several different meanings for the same word.

Analytical Thinking

Mary feared a world in which people would be made out of the organs and parts of the dead. Was she correct that this might someday happen? If so, list specific ways in which she was accurate in her predictions. To what extent has science gone further than she predicated? To what extent has it not gone as far? Also, what are some of the benefits of such procedures; what are some of the inherent dangers?

Descriptive Writing

A: Here is a list of objects that might be found in a laboratory like Dr. Frankenstein's. Notice that each involves one or more of the senses: sight, touch, taste, feel, smell, sound. Here are some examples:

❖ rotting, half-eaten food

❖ cobwebs which get on your clothing and skin

❖ a rusty iron vat filled with pungent, bubbling chemicals

❖ an ice-box filled with body parts

❖ stale air that causes bile to rise in your throat

❖ rank-smelling water dripping on you from the ceiling

❖ squealing pulleys for lifting heavy, unwieldy objects

❖ a steel table on which a corpse lies

❖ a foul and unnatural odor

❖ dirty, slimy surgical instruments

❖ squealing bats plastered with black scales to the walls and ceiling

❖ insects that buzz, bite, and attach themselves to your skin and clothing

Add at least seven more of your own, invoking as many of the senses as possible.

1. _____

2. _____

3. _____

4. _____

5. _____

6. _____

7. _____

B: Use at least five of your details in a paragraph describing the laboratory. Invoke as many senses as possible. Start with a solid, clear topic sentence; that is, fill in the blank with one or more adjectives of your own choosing that provides an overview of what you are going to emphasize about the laboratory; for example:

The doctor's laboratory was a _____ _____ place. (grimy, hideous, macabre, nauseating, bizarre, malodorous, terrifying, wretched)

As you write the body of your paragraph, focus on the details and where items are to be found in relation to one another. Create a clear, well-rounded picture (and sense) of the place—so that the reader can *see, feel, hear, taste, touch, and smell* it.

Creative Writing and Thinking

Writers and scientists have predicted many future occurrences and inventions. Some of these are listed below. After each, the beginning of a very short story is given. Write a disturbing, frightening ending to the story.

1. A substance enabling people to live forever

   After drinking the potion that would make her indestructible and give her eternal life, Susan went for a drive. As she raced along recklessly at a high speed, she suddenly....

2. Cloning

   Dr. Jeri Matthews, at age sixty, felt old and tired. Working alone late one night at the laboratory, she was surprised to hear a door open in the cellar and then the sound of many footsteps....

3. Overpopulation

   Darryl was extremely hungry. In the microwave over a(n)_____. Going to the window, he looked out and saw....

Library and Information-Seeking Skills

1. Find a timeline or overview of scientific or medical discoveries in the early 1800s. As traditional ways of thinking were challenged by new discoveries, a fear of the possibilities of science began to occur. Relate this fear of science to the story of Frankenstein. How does this tie in to modern films and books about aliens or rampant viruses?

2. Find two or more poems about love by Percy Bysshe Shelley, the husband of Mary Shelley. Memorize ten or more lines from a poem written by Percy Bysshe Shelley after 1814, the year they ran off together.

3. Fetal cell transplants, embryo research, growing of body parts and other topics in medical ethics are in the news. Research in newspapers, magazines, or online resources one of these topics or a similar current problem in medical ethics and relate it to the building of a man in the story of Frankenstein.

From *Great Stories Behind Famous Books.* Copyright © 1999 by Don L. Wulffson. (Alleyside Press, 1999)

Teacher Resources
Whole Language Activities for "The Birth of Frankenstein"

Before Writing Activities

Team Learning: Antonyms

The activity develops word and dictionary skills, and promotes the growth of social interaction skills, both cooperative and competitive. Some of the words are those which the students have encountered in previous selections or will encounter in forthcoming selections.

1. Divide the class into three or four teams. Identify them as Team 1, Team 2, Team 3, Team 4; appoint a leader/ spokesperson for each team.

2. Have the students number from 1 to 30 on their papers.

3. Say: "You are going to be working as teams in solving a word puzzle. You may use a dictionary, thesaurus, and any of the material from *Great Stories Behind Famous Books* to help you complete the activity. Though each member of every team will receive a worksheet, it is only the leader's paper I will examine."

4. Distribute the puzzles face-down. Tell students: "Once I give the word to begin, first write your name and team's number at the top. As soon as your team has finished, the leader will bring his or her paper to me for correction. I will mark right and wrong answers but give no clues. The team that finishes first will get an "A," that which finishes second will get a "B," and so on." (Or, use any technique consistent with your own grading system.)

5. Tell students: "Teamwork and good leadership are the key. Begin."

6. Once a correct sheet has been turned in, grade it, giving all members of the team the same grade. All worksheets must be filled out completely and correctly.

Antonyms

Add one letter to each word below—at the front, at the end, or anywhere inside—so that each numbered pair becomes two words that are opposite in meaning. *For example,* adding S and O to LOT and FUND in number 1 make LOST and FOUND.

1. lot — fund		16. hole — potion	
2. hut — hep		17. plum — sender	
3. sod — ought		18. moose — lithe	
4. had — ail		19. ascent — ding	
5. fail — roust		20. genus — moon	
6. modes — boatful		21. dead — ant	
7. sever — cement		22. maim — able	
8. vale — corn		23. base — nave	
9. aid — most		24. fees — purses	
10. spine — sanding		25. allow — panted	
11. covert — septic		26. pathetic — vita	
12. tarts — deists		27. pathetic — vial	
13. unposed — save		28. greed — reused	
14. over — covet		29. align — lad	
15. delete — hard		30. chase — defied	

Answers: (1) lost – found; (2) hurt – help; (3) sold – bought; (4) head – tail; (5) frail – robust; (6) modest – boastful; (7) severe – clement; (8) value – scorn; (9) arid – moist; (10) supine – standing; (11) convert – skeptic; (12) starts – desists; (13) unpoised – suave; (14) overt – covert; (15) deplete – hoard; (16) whole – portion; (17) plump – slender; (18) morose – blithe; (19) nascent – dying; (20) genius – moron; (21) dread – want; (22) maxim – fable; (23) blase – naïve; (24) flees – pursues; (25) fallow – planted; (26) apathetic – vital; (27) shack – palace; (28) malign – laud; (29) beget – kill; (30) chase – defied.

Comparative and Introspective Thinking

[Exercise sheet ☐]

The questions personalize the coming selection; that is, they encourage students to look within themselves at those aspects of their lives inducing anxiety. It is suggested that the activity be done orally so that each student can compare and contrast the similarities and differences in their anxieties and those of their peers. For item C, the essential difference is personal anxiety as opposed to concern for others.

Science Fiction [Exercise sheet ☐]

The goal here is to help students understand the essence of science fiction: prediction and prognostication of the future; fear of the future; preparation for the future, and avoidance of its looming dangers.

Vocabulary Development [Exercise sheet ☐]

The student learns to use context as a clue to word meaning.

During Reading Activities

The objective is for students, as they read, to prepare for discussion; that is, as they read, they learn to think critically and to anticipate an activity which should always be consequent to reading—review, analysis, and dialoguing.

After Reading Activities

Student Input

Via the above-mentioned activity, students should find that they are better prepared for discussion and other post-reading activities.

Analytical Thinking [Exercise sheet ☐]

Writers, especially the authors of sci-fi works, have, in essence, become modern-day prophets. Talk with students about other books, movies and plays that have, with varying degrees of success, predicted the future—and other works whose success in this prognostic venture remains to be seen.

Descriptive Writing [Exercise sheet ☐]

Learning to make one's writing "come alive" by invoking as many of the senses as possible.

Creative Writing and Thinking [Exercise sheet ☐]

Suggest that students write a story, poem, or play based on what they feel is their best response to the various paragraphs. In the holistic method of teaching, it is essential that the student be an active participant in the learning process. One method of approaching this activity is to write a play together with the class. The procedure is as follows:

1. The teacher reads some of the responses to "Creative Thinking and Writing," and the class decides/votes on the story line they like best.

2. The teacher begins the play on an overhead projector.

3. Calling for suggestions as to dialogue and continued narration, the teacher writes the play on the projector, as students copy it.

4. When completed, parts are assigned and the play is read aloud.

Library and Information-Seeking Skills

[Exercise sheet ☐]

1. A science and technology encyclopedia or a resource on the history of medicine should provide a good comparative timeline. An interesting challenge to the students would be to find a website containing this information.

2. There are many standard collections of Shelley's poetry that can be used as a resource for this question.

3. The key to this question is to select the best search term (medical ethics). You might introduce the students to the *Library of Congress Subject Headings* if your library has a copy.

Chapter 7

Night of Futility

Lord's *A Night to Remember*, and Other Works Concerning the *Titanic*

Morgan Andrew Robertson (1861–1915) was a popular American writer of romantic sea adventures. Born in Oswego, New York, the son of a ship's captain, he enlisted in the merchant marine at the age of sixteen. The next ten years of his life were spent on various ships, and this experience gave him the material for his fiction. In all, Robertson wrote more than two hundred stories of various length, a majority of which were reprinted in a collection of fourteen books.

Of all Robertson's works, his most historically significant is one entitled *Futility*. Like its author, you have probably never heard of it; the two wallow together in obscurity.

Futility is about the ill-fated voyage of a fabulous ocean liner, a ship far larger than any previously built. It is triple-screwed, made entirely of steel, and can travel at speeds up to twenty-five knots. On board are 3,000 people, among them some of the richest people on earth. Because of its many water-tight compartments and water-tight doors, the fictional ship is labeled "unsinkable." And largely because of its supposed invincibility, it carries far too few lifeboats.

In the story, the vessel is traveling at an excessive speed on a cold moonlit evening in April. Near midnight, the ship grazes an iceberg on its starboard side. With great loss of life, the unthinkable happens—the "unsinkable" ship goes down with appalling loss of life.

Mr. Robertson's novel, it would seem more than apparent, is about the tragic voyage of the *Titanic*. And like John Cameron's Oscar-winning motion picture of 1998 on the same subject, it is in the tra-dition of based-on-fact fiction. In the film, there is a highly unlikely occurrence: a romance between a first-class and a third-class passenger. In *Futility*, a seaman is thrown onto the iceberg, as is a little girl, whose life he saves.

Adding fanciful elements for dramatic effect are to be expected in works of this genre. However, there are other aspects of Mr. Robertson's book which are a bit baffling; in choosing the *Titanic* as his setting, he intentionally incorporated, it seems, a number of very obvious discrepancies in his story.

In *Futility*, he calls the ship the *Titan*. Why, when the ship is obviously the *Titanic*, would the author make this slight alteration of its name? Moreover, the *Titanic* traveled from Southampton, England, to New York. In his book, Robertson reverses this, and has the vessel traveling in the opposite direction, from New York to Southampton. Perhaps most inexplicable of all, the *Titanic* went down on her maiden voyage—certainly a fact which adds a grandly dramatic touch to the tragedy. Yet, when Mr. Robertson put pen to paper, he had the liner on her third round-trip across the Atlantic.

In addition to these idiosyncratic changes, there is another oddity about Morgan Robertson's work—quite a disturbing one. Until his dying day, he claimed that *Futility* was purely a work of fiction. The characters aboard the ship were not real people, and none of them died. As to the *Titan*, no such ship—or similar ship—had ever existed. In no way, he insisted, was his book historical.

And he was right!

You see, his novel was written in 1898. The *Titanic* sank in 1912. Morgan Robertson's book,

From *Great Stories Behind Famous Books*. Copyright © 1999 by Don L. Wulffson. (Alleyside Press, 1999)

written and published fourteen years before the tragedy, foretold, with shocking accuracy, an event that had yet to occur.

Sensationalistic—and nonsensical—tabloid articles soon hit the stands. Some suggested that Robertson was a prophet. Others, with a transparent veneer of scientific sophistication, used the writing as "proof" of the existence of ESP. Others, with an affinity for poor taste and hard-pressed for a new angle, intimated that Robertson was somehow responsible for the sinking of the *Titanic*, his motive being to stimulate massive sales of his book. Adding weight to this ill-founded, illegitimate claim was that, within months of the ship's sinking, the publisher reprinted *Futility*, its title—for conspicuously commercial reasons—changed to *The Wreck of the Titan*.

As for Morgan Robertson, the terrifying parallels of his fictional work with reality tormented him the rest of his life. A haunted, broken man, he died of alcoholism in 1915.

Forty years later, in 1955, an author by the name of Walter Lord wrote *A Night to Remember*, the first historically accurate and scholastically meritorious work on the sinking of the *Titanic*. The book has survived the test of time; it remains a relevant, poignant, but not overwrought accounting of what transpired on the night of April 14–15. There *are* unanswered questions in the work. For example: Were third-class passengers locked in lower compartments of the ship, assuring them of a watery death? Too, there are omissions and inaccuracies in the account; notably, the *Titanic* broke in half as she sank, which Mr. Lord does not mention.

These oversights, however, are quite understandable, and are surely not the consequence of poor research; the resting place of the *Titanic* was not discovered until 1985, thirty years after the writing of *A Night to Remember*. Since then, an extraordinary amount of information has come to light, as have thousands of artifacts—dolls, watches, paintings, cutlery. More, of course, will be found. Interestingly, it is within the realm of possibility that amidst this debris may be a book—a fictional story of a sea disaster, a work entitled *Futility*.

Student Assignment

Vocabulary Building Root Words

A root word is the base word from which other words, usually via compounding or the use of affixes, are derived. For example, the words inflammatory, flammable, flameproof, and flamboyant are derived from the word flame. For each list of words, determine its root word. (Notes: The root will *not* be one of the words in the list. Also, use a dictionary to help you.)

1. signify, signal, design, significantly

2. fabulous, fabulist, fabled, fable-prone

3. romaine, romantic , Roman, romanticize, unromantic

4. illegitimate, legality, legislate, legally, illegally

5. foretold, talk, telltale, talkative, tell, tale-spinner

6. unmerited, meritorious, demerit, meritocracy

7. insensitive, sensory, senselessness, unsensational

8. motivation, immovable, motive, moviegoer, removable

Fact or Opinion?

1. Morgan Robertson was a fine writer.

2. In all, Robertson wrote more than 200 stories of various length.

3. The *Titanic* set sail from Southampton, England, for New York.

4. Morgan Robertson was a prophet.

5. Some people suggested that Morgan Robertson was a prophet.

6. The ship was triple-screwed and made entirely of steel.

7. In 1955, Walter Lord wrote *A Night to Remember*.

8. The book is the first historically accurate and scholastically meritorious work on the subject.

9. The ship was labeled "unsinkable."

10. Adding fanciful elements for dramatic effect are to be expected in works of this genre.

Reading for Detail (Cooperative Learning)

1. Write ten fill-in-the-blank questions concerned with the selection.

   For example: The *Titanic* hit an iceberg in the month of _____, in the year _____.

2. When you finish writing your questions, exchange papers with another student (who also has finished writing his/her questions). Write:

   Answered by _(your name)_____

   at the bottom of the paper.

3. When you finish answering the questions, again exchange papers. You and the other student should correct each other's work and turn it in to the teacher.

Evaluation and Comparison

1. Think about the article you have just read. As is, not until you are approximately two-thirds through the article does the author reveal that *Futility* was written many years before the sinking of the *Titanic*. This information is crucial—and is, by and large, the theme and thrust of the selection. In your opinion, why did the author wait so long before divulging this information? Did doing so improve the article or weaken it? Explain.

2. Write an opening to the selection which tells up front what it is about. That is, in from one to three paragraphs, tell the reader from the very start that your article is about a book written before the sinking of the *Titanic* that parallels the disaster and seemingly foretells its occurrence.

3. What is the appeal of *A Night to Remember*, and other such works which tell the actual story of the Titanic—its construction, its crossing of the Atlantic, and the tragic night on which it sank? Why does a work such as *A Night to Remember* make for compelling reading?

4. There have been numerous fictional works about disasters and near-disasters—for example: *Black Sunday, The Last Days of the Late, Great State of California, Plague,* and *Nineteen Eighty-Four*. What is the appeal of works such as these? In what ways is their appeal different from that of nonfiction works?

Thinking Objectively

The parallels between *Futility* and the actual sinking of the *Titanic* are startling. However, to a degree, some of them can be explained as coincidence. Also, one must keep in mind that Robertson, in conjuring up a novel about a sea disaster, simply made logical choices about details of the disaster—choices that you probably would have made if you were plotting the story. To see how this works, answer the following questions.

1. Which is more dramatic, having a small ocean liner sink or a huge one?

2. Look up the words *large* or *size* in a thesaurus. Make a list of words meaning "huge."

3. Which is more dramatic (and ironic), the sinking of an old, obsolete ship or one that, at

that time, was a state-of-the-art vessel? That is, would it be made of iron, wood, or steel? Would it have multiple propellers (screws), or just one? Would it be a fast ship? Would it contain modern safety devices—such as water-tight doors and compartments?

4. If a ship is going to go down on the open seas, what are some of the things that might cause this to happen?

5. The time of greatest peril of hitting an iceberg would be in early spring when the warm weather starts to melt polar ice, causing icebergs to detach and float south. Thus, what are the months in which such a collision would be most likely?

Creative Thinking and Writing

A: A significant amount of modern literature is based on predicting the future. Essentially, the author asks himself "what if" questions. For example: What if there were a second civil war in the United States?

Write out the following questions inserting words of your choice in the blanks. The words should create interesting and imaginative "what if?" scenarios for works of fiction.

1. What if the tomb of _____ was discovered?

2. What if all the water on earth _____ _____?

3. What if _____ were found to still be alive?

4. What if a newspaper writer began writing _____ _____?

5. What if all the _____ on earth were rendered sterile?

6. What if the White House_____ _____?

7. What if it were discovered that_____ was below the city of Dallas, Texas?

8. What if a girl was born who _____ _____?

9. What if scientists discovered a way to make trees that_____?

10. What if an insurance salesman had the ability to _____?

B: Write a short story or play based on the scenario above which most appeals to you.

Library and Information-Seeking Skills

1. The White Star Line had another ship, a sister ship to the *Titanic*, which also sank. Find the name of this ship and the story of its sinking. Why does the sinking of the *Titanic* overshadow this later sinking? Write paragraphs about each of the two ships and their disasters.

2. Find literary criticism of Walter Lord's book, *A Night to Remember* (1955). What was said about it at the time of publication? Or, find film reviews of James Cameron's movie *Titanic* (1998). What was said in the reviews about the historical accuracy or inaccuracy of the film? If you looked for both, which information was easier to find and why?

3. Find the names of two (or more) books and two to three magazine articles about the *Titanic* disaster written since the discovery of the site of the wreck. Check the Internet to find two websites that appear to have accurate information about the *Titanic* when compared to your other sources. Create a bibliography of these sources using standard bibliographic format.

4. Use any or all of the above resources to find biographical information about Walter Lord. Write a brief paragraph about him, including his reasons for writing about the *Titanic* disaster.

From *Great Stories Behind Famous Books*. Copyright © 1999 by Don L. Wulffson. (Alleyside Press, 1999)

Teacher Resources
Whole Language Activities for
"Night of Futility"

Before Reading Activities

Vocabulary Building Root Words [Exercise sheet ☐]

The purpose of the activity is for students to see the morphemic and etymological relationship of words. More importantly, it provides them with a vehicle whereby they can readily expand and enhance their vocabularies.

Answers: (1) sign; (2) fable; (3) Rome; (4) legal; (5) merit; (6) sense; (7) move.

Fact or Opinion? [Exercise sheet ☐]

It is essential that students learn to differentiate fact from opinion in what they read. Point out that this is pertinent not only to literature, but also to so many of their daily encounters. For example, the opinions of their peers, of politicians, and others are relentlessly delivered as though they are facts. Most conspicuous, perhaps, is the use of this "technique" in advertising; thus, as homework, have students cut out ads and find opinions (and statements) proffered as facts.

During Reading Activities

Conjecture and Critical Thinking

Before distributing copies of the story, read the story aloud to the class. Stop reading at the end of the eighth paragraph (which begins: "In addition to these idiosyncratic changes …" and ends with: "In no way, he insisted, was his book historical." Ask the class these questions:

1. Does this last paragraph indicate that Robertson may have been of unsound mind, perhaps insane?

2. Is it possible that he was correct, that his story, for some reason, was *not* historical? Explain.

3. Read the following: "In no way, he insisted, was his book historical. And he was right!" Ask students how the statement that "he was right"

alters their perception of Robertson and possible reasons for the numerous discrepancies between Robertson's work and the actual sinking of the *Titanic*. Ask if the statement "And he was right!" is one which needs explaining, and how important that explanation is to the article as a whole.

After Reading Activities

Reading for Detail (Cooperative Learning)

[Exercise sheet ☐]

The activity, in keeping with "whole language," continues to make young people active participants in the learning process and to instill in them the notion that they are—in all respects—part of the learning process, which includes assuming the role of a teacher.

Evaluation and Comparison [Exercise sheet ☐]

1. The intent of writing the article in the manner it was done was to add an element of surprise. However, students may have legitimate reasons for not liking the technique. Discuss both the good and bad aspects of this technique of presentation.

2. The activity develops writing skill, and allows the student to compare and contrast writing techniques in an active rather than a passive manner.

3. The essence of the activity is comparing the appeal of fiction versus nonfiction. Discuss with students their preference for either fictional or nonfictional works.

Thinking Objectively

Though it is fascinating that a work of fiction presaged real incident, it would, however, be a disservice to young people not to demystify the occurrence, or at least attempt to do so. Some students may ultimately conclude that supernatural, psychic, or mystical forces

From *Great Stories Behind Famous Books.* Copyright © 1999 by Don L. Wulffson. (Alleyside Press, 1999)

were at work. That is their prerogative; however, before doing so they have at least attempted to look at this eventuality in a logical and rational manner—and, hopefully, will continue to exercise this modus operandi in the future.

Creative Thinking and Writing [Exercise sheet ☐]

In addition to promoting creative thinking and writing, we have also provided the students with a valuable tool which can be applied to other such endeavors. That is, the students are now equipped with a very useful method of getting started with their writing—the nemesis of not only nascent writers but of accomplished authors. Moreover, in their continuing study of literature, the student can apply this question to most works they read in order to understand the geneses of story lines and plots.

Library and Information-Seeking Skills

[Exercise sheet ☐]

1. Suggest that the students search other reference books on maritime disasters, using the White Star Line as a basic search term.

2. *Book Review Digest* and *The Readers' Guide to Periodical Literature* are two of the best commonly available resources to answer this question.

3. *The Readers' Guide* is available in both print and electronic formats, and through licensing agreements, it is also accessible on the web.

4. In addition to the aforecited resources, author information can also be located in other Wilson publications such as *Wilson Biographies, World Authors,* and *Current Biography.*

Chapter 8

Of Mice and Men

Steinbeck

John Steinbeck was a shy man. Speaking on the phone frightened him, as did speaking before a group. Even when he had achieved fame as a writer, he almost never granted interviews. He did not feel comfortable around others, even with his friends. Instead of talking to them, he wrote them letters.

His favorite instrument was the pencil. Every morning he would obsessively sharpen exactly twenty-four pencils—one for each hour of the coming day. Then he would do what he loved best: write. Tirelessly, endlessly—and contentedly—he wrote, always in a tiny script, usually on yellow, legal-size pads. Later in life, he finally let go of his pencils, and instead carefully tapped out his letters and prose on a typewriter. In his lifetime, he literally wrote thousands upon thousands of letters, a collection of short stories, sixteen novels, and two screenplays.

The setting of most of Steinbeck's books is Northern California, near the towns of Monterey and Salinas, his birthplace. His mother was a schoolteacher, his father a farmer. In coming from a working-class background, his fiction is peopled with characters who struggle hard to make a living and for whom the future holds no guarantees. Before finally being able to support himself with his writing, Steinbeck worked as a fisherman, ranch hand, farmer, fruit picker, and bricklayer.

In 1920, he entered Stanford University. Though he remained there for five years, he was an indifferent student and never acquired a degree. Only rarely did he make an appearance in class; instead, he spent his time in his room, writing story after story and sending them off to publishers. All were rejected.

In 1925, he left Stanford mid-semester, and eventually made his way to New York. There, by day he worked as a laborer on the construction of Madison Square Garden; at night and on weekends, he wrote, and continued to gather rejection slips.

After returning to California, in 1929 Steinbeck published his first novel, *Cup of Gold*. The book was a flop; it failed even to earn back the $250 the publisher had given the author as an advance. "It doesn't matter," he wrote in a letter. "I don't expect to write anything important until my fifth book."

His fifth book almost never came to pass. He had almost finished the work, when, one night, while he and his wife were out, their Irish Setter puppy found the manuscript and destroyed more than half of it. It took Steinbeck almost three months to recreate the missing parts.

While rewriting the book, the author changed its title. All along he had been calling it *Something That Happened*. In the opening scene, a retarded man is playing with a dead mouse, caressing it lovingly; moreover, a central motif of the story is the futility of our hopes and dreams. A poem the author knew and loved well came to mind, a poem by Robert Burns, which includes the lines "The best laid plans of mice and men/Often go awry."

John Steinbeck's fifth book was *Of Mice and Men*. Published in 1937, it was surely "important." And it was more. *Of Mice and Men* is a masterpiece of storytelling.

The story begins as it ends.

In the beginning, two men, migrant workers, are sitting by a stream. The two are an odd pair—George: A small man with a quick mind. Lennie: A huge man with a slow mind. Each fills a void in the other's life. Lennie, retarded, depends on George for guidance. George, a man going nowhere in life, finds purpose and meaning in his day-to-day existence by taking care of Lennie. A curious bond—unusual, strange. But still a loving one. Too, the men share a dream: someday they will have a little place of their own. As they sit there, George talks—telling Lennie about this magical, wonderful place—where someday they will settle down and be happy.

In the morning the two leave the haven of the stream and head to a ranch, where a job awaits them. The place is only a means to an end. There they hope to earn a "grub stake," enough money to purchase their dream. They do not know, of course, that the ranch to which they are heading, instead of the source of the fulfillment of their dream, will be the source of its destruction.

After three days at the ranch, powerful, dull-witted Lennie accidentally kills a woman. He flees in a panic, with the other ranch hands hot on his trail. He is not sure what he has done; he cannot really remember it. He knows only that George will be mad at him.

A thematic circle is completed: Lennie returns to where the story began; and there his friend George finds him—sitting by the stream in the quiet woods. Instead of anger, George feels only compassion for Lennie. He comforts him as best he can. He tells him about the happy future they will share. He then asks Lennie to look across the stream and imagine the place they will someday have—their wonderful, magical dream home. Lennie smiles. George continues talking about their plans until he hears the others approaching. To spare Lennie the unbearable, terrifying torment that awaits him, and in a final act of love, George puts a pistol to his friend's head and pulls the trigger.

In killing Lennie, George kills his own dream. As he often expresses in the story, no dream can exist unless it is shared. Too, if we subscribe to a motif portrayed in many works (e.g., *Dr. Jekyll & Mr. Hyde*) Lennie and George can be seen as the two parts of one man. George is the mind; Lennie is the body. Neither can exist apart; to kill either half is to kill the whole.

Steinbeck's language and style are natural, unadorned, and direct, his sentences carefully constructed. His characters are simple people—the below-average, the down-trodden, the dispossessed. Still, as we all do, they have their dreams. And as it happens for many of us, their dreams, and they as people, are destroyed in part by society; but even more so, they are defeated by their own limitations, the flaws inherent in their personalities

This, then, is the tragedy of George and Lennie. And to echo Steinbeck's original title for the book, in its modest, subdued tone, and its suggestion of resignation to forces beyond our control, what befell George is Lennie. It is simply "something that happened."

From *Great Stories Behind Famous Books*. Copyright © 1999 by Don L. Wulffson. (Alleyside Press, 1999)

Student Assignment

Personal Analysis: Your Dreams and Goals

1. What are some of your dreams and goals in life? What obstacles stand in the way of their achievement? What essential steps must you take in trying to achieve them?

2. Have any of your previous hopes and dreams been dashed? If so, how? Why?

3. What differences do you see between the following dreams? Setting up a refuge for abused and abandoned animals. Having a small, peaceful farm. Becoming a successful writer. Owning several factories and becoming wealthy.

Without giving names, the teacher will read some of the answers to item 1 above aloud.

Evaluative and Extrapolative Thinking

1. Why did George kill Lennie? Was it the right thing to do? Would you have done the same?

2. In the book, an old man has an old, infirm, and almost-blind dog. The animal has outlived its usefulness, except as a loving companion to the old man; too, the animal smells bad, a fact which bothers the ranch hands. The old man is persuaded, coerced, really, into having his dog killed. What parallel do you see between the killing of Lennie and the dog?

3. Why do you think the author chose to have the story begin and end at the same place? Could it be said that the place is both a place of life and death.

4. When George discusses his plans for the future, two other hands on the ranch want to be a part of it—and join Lennie and George. Why? Under the circumstances, would you have wanted to join them?

5. Sigmund Freud, the famous psychoanalyst, has said there are two major components of each the person—the ego and the id. The id is that part of the psyche which is regarded as a reservoir of our instinctive drives; it is dominated by the pleasure principle. The ego is the rational part of our being and that which governs and guides action. Compare Lennie and George in these psychoanalytic terms.

6. Could it be said that George and Lennie, symbolically, are two halves of one man?

7. The superego is another Freudian term referring to that part of the psyche which is critical of the ego and enforces moral standards upon it. Where in the story, if at all, does George's superego come into play?

8. Discuss what you think George's life would be like without Lennie, and vice-versa.

9. Do you feel sympathetic toward George, toward Lennie? Discuss this.

10. How might the saying, "are you a man or a mouse?" relate to the book?

From Great Stories Behind Famous Books. Copyright © 1999 by Don L. Wulffson. (Alleyside Press, 1999)

Characterization

Below are some of the devices an author uses to develop and reveal character. What do each of the quotes reveal about George?

1. What the character says:

    a) [George to the old man]

    "You was pokin' your big ears into our business. I don't like nobody to get nosey."

    b) George said, "I'm stayin' right here. I don't want to get mixed up in nothing. Lennie and me got to make a stake."

    c) [George and Lennie had arrived at the ranch and were talking to the boss about a job.]

    George broke in loudly. "Oh! I ain't saying he's bright. He ain't. But I say he's a damn good worker."

2. The setting where we find the character:

    The bunk house [where they would be living] was a long, rectangular building... Against the walls were eight bunks, five of them made up with blanket and the other three showing their burlap ticking.

3. What others say to the character

    [The boss said to George,] All right. "But don't try to put nothing over, 'cause you can't get away with nothing. I seen wise guys before."

4. What the character does

    [George] unrolled his bindle and put things on the shelf, his razor and bar of soap, his bomb and bottle of pills, his liniment and leather wristband. He made his bed up neatly with blankets.

5. The actions of the character and how others react to him

    George's hand remained outstretched imperiously. Slowly, like a terrier who doesn't want to bring a ball to its master, Lennie approached, drew back, approached again. George snapped his fingers sharply, and at the sound Lennie laid the mouse in his hand.

6. The appearance of the character

    [George was] dressed in denim trousers and a denim coat with brass buttons. On his head was a black, shapeless hat and [he] carried a tight blanket roll slung over his shoulder. He was a small and quick man, dark of face, with restless eyes and sharp, strong features. Every part of him was defined: small, strong hands, slender arms, a thin and bony nose.

Writing

Write a story, play, or essay (or even a poem or cartoon) in which one of the "moral decision" questions is the main conflict and the writer is the main character. Start with a line as simple as:

I was walking down the street, headed to...

Library and Information-Seeking Skills

1. Research the setting of the stories of Steinbeck—near Monterey and Salinas, California. Describe the geography and climate of the area. Describe the major events of the 1920s in the United States, which encompassed Steinbeck's college years through the publication of his first book.

2. Research the history of migrant workers in California from the 1920s to the current date. What has changed since the 1920s? What has remained the same? What were their economic conditions then and now? What were their living conditions then, and what are they like now?

3. Use a poetry index to find the Robert Burns poem which contains the line:

    The best laid plans of mice and men
    Often go awry.

    Write a paragraph about what the poem means to you.

Teacher Resources
Whole Language Activities for "Of Mice and Men"

Note: The activities are formulated in such a manner that *Of Mice and Men* may be approached in two ways by the class and teacher. Because of its ubiquity in secondary language arts curricula, and because it is both a fast and poignant read, the work can be an assigned class-reading experience; and as such, the following activities can be used to augment students' comprehension of the work. At the same time, the material is presented in such a way that the student, via completion of all the activities, will (even without reading the book) come away with a rather complete and well-rounded understanding of the story—its style, plot, characters, and themes. The usage of the activities—and the order of their use—will depend upon the decision as to whether or not to assign the book as a whole-class reading experience.

Before Reading Activities

Personal Analysis: Your Dreams and Goals
[Exercise sheet ☐]
The goal of the activity is for the student to personalize literature; that is, to identify with the characters, and in the case of George and Lennie, to empathize with their hopes and dreams, successes and failures.

Moral Decisions
The activity promotes speaking and social interaction skills, and supports personal growth. Moreover, it prepares the student for the reading selection that follows as well as for the writing activity.

Directions
Part A

1. Have the students take out a piece of paper and number from 1 through 16.

2. Say: "Each of you is going to be asked a question calling for a moral decision on your part. That is, presented with a difficult situation, what choice would you make? When asked, do not give your answer immediately; instead, write it on a piece of paper. As you do, everyone in class will write down your name and how they think you will answer."

3. Ask the first question of the first student (choosing a person who tends to be outgoing). Tell the student that he or she has the option of writing an answer that varies from the choices offered.

4. After the student has written a response, and everyone else has written their guess as to the response, ask for a show of hands as to how the class believes the person has answered.

5. Now, ask the person for his or her actual answer, permitting the student to explain their choice if he or she desires.

6. The class marks their guesses as right or wrong.

Questions:

1. You see someone steal an old lady's purse. Do you …

   a) Go after the thief?
   b) Call 911?
   c) Do nothing?

2. Someone tells you that the person you're going with is cheating on you. Do you …

   a) Dump the person?
   b) Ask the person you're going with to explain or defend himself or herself?
   c) Snoop and do a little detective work to find out whether or not it's true?

3. You see a blind man who desperately needs help getting across the street just as your bus arrives to take you to school. If you're late to class, you know you will get detention and fail a test. No one else is around to help the man? Do you …

   a) Help him?

From *Great Stories Behind Famous Books.* Copyright © 1999 by Don L. Wulffson. (Alleyside Press, 1999)

b) Get on the bus?

4. You are renting out a spare room in your house. A terribly deformed and ugly man asks to rent the room. Do you …

   a) Tell him to leave?

   b) Tell him it's already rented?

   c) Rent the room to him?

5. A sickly looking man passes out in the street and stops breathing. Do you …

   a) Call 911?

   b) Give the man mouth-to-mouth CPR?

   c) Give the man CPR—but without mouth-to-mouth resuscitation?

   d) Do nothing?

6. You are offered $1,000 to pose in the nude in a magazine. Would you …

   a) Refuse?

   b) Accept?

7. A woman is screaming that someone is trying to kill her, and she is beating on your door and begging you to let her in. Do you …

   a) Call 911, but not let her in?

   b) Let her in?

   c) Ignore her pleas?

8. While driving your parents' car, which you're not allowed to do, you accidentally hit another car with your bumper. The other car is dented badly, but yours hardly has a scratch. Do you …

   a) Leave a note under the windshield wiper of the other car (as required by law)?

   b) Drive off without leaving a note, hoping no one saw you or got your license number?

9. A bully threatens to beat you up unless you do his (or *her*) homework. Do you …

   a) Tell the teacher or another person about the threat?

   b) Simply refuse to do what the bully demands?

   c) Do the bully's homework?

   d) Fight the bully?

10. You see a poor-looking old man drop his wallet. Do you …

    a) Take the wallet and cash?

    b) Return the wallet and money to the old man?

    c) Ignore the dropped wallet?

11. You see a wealthy-looking man drop his wallet. Do you …

    a) Take the wallet and cash?

    b) Return the wallet and money to the man?

    c) Ignore the dropped wallet?

12. While walking alone, you see a cat hit by a car. It's alive but in pain. Do you …

    a) Ignore the cat?

    b) Try to help it?

    c) Try to get others to help?

13. As you are walking toward where your friends are standing, a retarded girl (whom you do not know) comes up alongside you. She wants to walk with you and talk. Your friends are coming into view. Do you …

    a) Hurry away from the retarded girl?

    b) Walk and talk with her?

    c) Tell her to go away?

14. A loved one is dying in agony of an incurable disease and asks you to help him or her commit suicide. Do you …

    a) Assist in the suicide?

    b) Try to talk the person out of it?

    c) Call a doctor?

    d) Do nothing?

15. The teacher of a class you are near failing drops her grade-book. Do you …

    a) Give it back?

    b) Change or raise some of your grades, then give it back?

    c) Throw it away?

    d) Leave it where it was dropped?

Part B

Say: "Write one original question regarding making a moral choice. You will be asking your question of anyone in class (including the teacher!).

Part C

After the students have had time to write their questions, call on them one at a time to ask their question of anyone they choose.

Part D

Have the students write a story in which one of the moral-decision questions is used as the main conflict and the writer is the main character. Tell them that they can start with a line as simple as: *I was walking dow the street, headed to…*

Tell the students they can do the assignment as a play, short story, poem, or even a cartoon. Also, if a question was based on a true incident, students may do the assignment as a personal narrative. (The writing may be done as a "Before Reading" or "After Reading" activity.)

During Reading Activities

Flexible Thinking

Read the selection aloud to students. Stop after reading paragraph three. Say: "The author of this selection describes George and Lennie as 'an odd pair.' George is a small man with a quick mind; Lennie, a huge man with a slow mind.' What does the author give for the reason the two men are companions? What other possible reasons can you give for the two men to want to be companions? Again, stop after reading paragraph four. Ask students: "What do you think the author meant when he wrote: "They do not know … that the ranch to which they are heading, instead of the source of the fulfillment of their dream, will be the source of its destruction"? What do you think might happen at the ranch that might destroy their dream?

After Reading Activities

Evaluative and Extrapolative Thinking

[Exercise sheet ☐]

The purpose of this activity is encourage the students to analyze the actions of the characters in relationship to the various motifs of the story and to promote awareness of the storyteller's purpose, technique, and artistry.

Characterization   [Exercise sheet ☐]

The activity familiarizes students with the basic techniques of characterization. Moreover, via this familiarization, we enhance their skill in analyzing and understanding fictional characters.

Writing [Exercise sheet ☐]

Essential to the development of writing skill is for students to recognize that everyday problems and conflicts are the essence of literature. And this includes *their* everyday travails, *their* hopes and dreams, *their* successes and failures. It is extremely important that students recognize that it is in *their own lives* that they can find the stuff—the material—for effective written expression—that is, writing of interest to others.

Library and Information-Seeking Skills

[Exercise sheet ☐]

1. The best resources for this information will be either a book on the history of the U.S. during the 1920s or a CD-ROM. Emphasize the importance of a good index in selecting research tools for this type of assignment.

2. If the students select an electronic reference resource, encourage them to practice their skills in Boolean search techniques, linking several terms to refine their search.

3. Besides *Bartlett's*, there are several other poetry indexes that will supply this answer, including *The Oxford Dictionary of Quotations.*

Chapter 9

The Woman in White

Dickinson

The townspeople of Amherst, Massachusetts, called her "the woman in white."

She was small, her skin alabaster, her hair black and primly tied back, her voice nervous, breathy, fluttery. And with her large, fearful eyes, and rather homely, sharp-featured countenance, to many she looked like a bird, "like a wren," perhaps.

Odd. To her neighbors she seemed incredibly odd, and not just because of her looks. It was that she was such a solitary creature, a recluse, a woman so frightened of the world that she lived in hiding; a being shrouded in mystery, she lived alone. And then there was the matter of how she dressed. She never married, and seemed uninterested in the prospect, yet for some unfathomable reason, she always wore white.

As though she were a bride unto herself.

The "woman in white" had been born in 1830 in Amherst, in a large, stately brick house—a mansion, really, which had been built by her grandfather. The place was across the street from a cemetery.

During her life, only on a few rare occasions did she leave the house—most notably, in 1847, to attend college, Mount Holyoke Female Seminary. Initially, she was enthusiastic. Her enthusiasm paled: she found traditionalist academia stifling, and though religious, she found her beliefs at odds with the tenets of orthodox Protestant Christianity. She returned home, to her family, and to her private ways.

The years passed.

She tended to her aging, ailing parents; and when they passed away, she continued on there, in strange, complacent solitude. Occasionally she would receive visitors; but as her isolation became more intense, more phobic, she would only do so in a truly queer manner. Her guests would sit downstairs; she would sit upstairs, in her own room, and through an ajar door, heard but not seen, she would converse with those below.

Her relationship with children was conducted in much the same manner. Fond of children, from her upstairs window she would sometimes wave to them, beckon them. At their approach, she would lower a basket; in it would be preserves, pastries, fruit, and home-made candy. Then she would raise the basket and retreat into the shadowy confines of the house.

Only very early in the morning and then at twilight was she ever seen outdoors. Alone, immaculately dressed in white, she would quietly wander the spacious grounds surrounding the house, her manner thoughtful, pensive, reflective, as though spellbound by the minutest details of nature. Of nature, she seemed in awe; and wholly at peace, wholly content to be amidst that little part of it she could claim as her own.

Were a neighbor to pass by, she would pretend not to notice, or sometimes she would hide behind a tree or shrubbery. Strangers would send her into a panic, send her fleeing indoors to the emotional safety of her home.

At night, the place looked as dark and desolate as a tomb. Sometimes, lamp in hand, the spectral silhouette of a woman would pass the lace-curtained windows. Other times, a form could be made out in the upstairs bedroom; alone, almost immobile, seated at a desk, it appeared she was writing, or something of the sort.

"She is so peculiar, such a strange one," the towns-

From *Great Stories Behind Famous Books*. Copyright © 1999 by Don L. Wulffson. (Alleyside Press, 1999)

people would say of her. "She does nothing—nothing but hide from the world. Such a wasted life!"

When, in 1886, at the age of 56, the "woman in white" died, no one really knew her; and outside of Amherst, hardly a person had even been aware of her existence. The name Emily Dickinson meant absolutely nothing to them.

Among her personal effects and private papers were these handwritten words:

I'm nobody! Who are you?
Are you—Nobody—too?

Her entire life, to the world, and in her own eyes, Emily Dickinson had been a "nobody." The vicissitudes of circumstance had forced this existence of anonymous seclusion upon her; and then too, she had chosen it, preferred it. For she had also written:

How dreary to be somebody
How public, like a frog …

One thousand seven hundred and seventy-five poems! That is what Ms. Dickinson left for the world. Her sister Lavinia found them, most of them in a large wooden chest in Emily's upstairs room. In tidy little collections of verse—manuscript packets of a few sheets each of folded stationery, threaded at the spine, she wrote of life as she saw it. In quiet defiance of the accepted conventions of meter and rhyme, she explored her own psyche, proffered gentle insights into the human soul, and embraced the timeless mysteries of life and death.

Of her hundreds of poems, only seven were published while Emily Dickinson was alive—and these without her knowledge or consent. She sought no audience but herself; in almost total artistic isolation, she relied entirely on the purity of her own vision and creativity. Unsullied by the opinions of others of her time, untouched in her solitude, Emily Dickinson—"the woman in white"—was able to leave to the world poetry that is, without question, wholly unique, singularly powerful, and truly timeless.

Student Assignment

Before Reading Activities

Vocabulary: Synonyms

First, unscramble the words at the left. Second, match each with the word at the right which is closest in meaning.

1.	a c l a	immaculate
2.	r e d c v o e	complacent
3.	u e f f a r l	phobic
4.	n l a c e	shrouded
5.	m a l l s	countenance
6.	c a f e	beckon
7.	l i b s e f e	alabaster
8.	y a p h p	minute
9.	o e a n l	tenets
10.	t h i w e	solitary

After Reading Activities

Analytical and Comparative Thinking

In reading "The Woman in White" you learned a number of things about the life of Emily Dickinson—her beliefs, her personal tragedies, her fears, her joys, and so forth. The following are several excerpts from her poetry, all of which are similarly revealing. What does each excerpt reveal about her, and to what in her life does it refer? Too, how does the revelation in the poem coincide with what you learned from reading "The Woman in White"?

1. I'll tell you how the sun rose,—
   A ribbon at a time …

From *Great Stories Behind Famous Books.* Copyright © 1999 by Don L. Wulffson. (Alleyside Press, 1999)

2. I reckon—when I count at all—
   First—Poets—Then the Sun—
   Then Summer—Then the Heaven of God—
   And then—-the list is done.

3. The soul unto itself
   Is an imperial friend,—

4. If I can stop one heart from breaking,
   I shall not live in vain;

5. There is no frigate like a book
   To take us lands away …

6. I've seen a dying eye
   Run round and round a room
   In search of something, as it seemed,
   Then cloudier become …

7. Afraid? Of whom am I afraid?
   Not death; for who is he?
   …Of life? 'Twere odd I fear a thing
   That comprehendeth me …

8. The Bible is an antique volume
   Written by faded men …

Analysis, Understanding and Evaluation

Dickinson's poetry did not conform to the nineteenth century notion of poetry—verse that adhered to regular meter and rhyme. Moreover, her word choice, punctuation, and grammar defy convention; her metaphors are unusual, and frequently surprising; her message is often convoluted and ambiguous, seemingly intentionally.

After great pain a formal feeling comes—
The nerves sit ceremonious like tombs;
The stiff Heart questions—was it He that bore?
And yesterday—or centuries before?

The feet, mechanical, go round
A wooden way
Of ground, or air, or ought,
Regardless grown,
A quartz contentment, like a stone.

This is the hour of lead
Remembered if outlived,
As freezing persons recollect the snow—
First chill, then stupor, then the
letting go.

1. Look up the words assonance and dissonance in a dictionary. List examples you find in the above poem.

2. Dickinson utilizes what is known as "off-rhyme" or "imperfect rhyme." Basically, this is the use of words which, in terms of sound, do not match perfectly (e.g., fall/call). What examples of "off-rhyme" do you find in this poem?

3. What examples do you see of unusual word choice, punctuation, and grammar?

4. What metaphors do you see? What word(s) would you use to describe these metaphors?

5. What, in your opinion, is this poem about? What is happening?

   What does it make you hear, feel, see, smell, and taste? What is the mood? How does it make you feel?

6. What is your opinion of the poem? What do you like about it? What do you dislike?

From *Great Stories Behind Famous Books.* Copyright © 1999 by Don L. Wulffson. (Alleyside Press, 1999)

Word Choice and Imagery

Dickinson very frequently chose unexpected, unusual words, and in so doing created very powerful images. In each of the blanks below, put an out-of-the-ordinary word—or words—in order to create strong, distinctive word-pictures.

1. Fear _____ upon a _____ of thorns

2. I_____ a rose made of _____, and then _____ beside it

3. The only _____ I ever held was dressed in _____ and _____

Creative Writing

Continue one or more of the above lines to create a poem. Or, as did Dickinson, write a poem in any manner or style of your own choosing.

Library and Information-Seeking Skills

1. Use two standard English literature resources or encyclopedia entries or online resources to compare and contrast the lives of Emily Dickinson and Jane Austen. How did their intense focus on a small part of life lead to literary respect? Try these websites:

   www.planet.net/pkrisxle/emily/dickinson.html
   (Emily Dickinson)

   andromeda.rutgers.edu/~jlynch/Lit/american.html
   (Literary Resources—American)

2. Using a medical or psychology dictionary or encyclopedia, find the definition and symptoms of agoraphobia. Use a dictionary to find the definitions of reclusive and eccentric. In what ways do these terms remind you of Emily Dickinson? Can you think of any modern public figures who could be considered eccentric or reclusive?

3. Emily Dickinson's poems are often quoted. Check a quotation collection, such as *Bartlett's* or another, to find quotes from her poems. Find two you could possibly use as part of your e-mail signature or as a sign on your wall or binder.

Teacher Resources
Whole Language Activities for
"The Woman in White"

Before Reading Activities

Vocabulary: Synonyms [Exercise sheet ☐]
The goal is to familiarize students with words they will be encountering in the selection.

Pre-Reading Activity

In addition to preparing the student for the reading selection to come, the activity suggests the students' commonality with the writers with whom they are dealing (as well as with their classmates). In holistic teaching it is less important that the student adulate famous writers than it is that they see the essential human sameness between themselves and those they study. Therefore, they respect—and understand—these writers more fully, and at the same time learn to respect—as well as better understand—themselves.

Before beginning, the teacher should read the following and fill in the blanks with something that is "public" about yourself and something that is "private." For example, a public fact might be that you have curly hair; a private fact might be that you are terrified of snakes, lost your mother when you were three, or that you collect autographs.

1. Say: "All of us have a public and a private self. For example, you probably have noticed that I _____, which is part of my public self. However, you probably don't know that I _____, which is part of my private self."

2. Say: "On a sheet of paper write the word public and the word private. (Do not give your name.)" When students finish, collect the papers and read their answers aloud.

3. Tell them that the selection they are going to be reading is about someone in which the concept of public versus private self plays an extremely important role.

During Reading Activity

1. Read the first paragraph aloud, then call on students to read subsequent paragraphs.

2. Have students read the selection silently. As they read, have them list three aspects of Dickinson's life which were public and three which were private. When students have finished writing, discuss their answers and write them on the board. Point out that they share with Dickinson (and other writers) an inner and outer self.

After Reading Activities
Analytical and Comparative Thinking

[Exercise sheet ☐]
The goal is that students discover the direct interaction between an author's life-history (personality, personal circumstance, habits, etc.) and the works they produce, not only in general but also in terms of specific works—and even specific passages.

Analysis, Understanding and Evaluation

[Exercise sheet ☐]
As Dickinson's acquaintance Thomas Higginson wrote of her poetry, "What place ought to be assigned in literature to what is so remarkable, yet so elusive of criticism." Nevertheless, it is important to acquaint students with the basics of her techniques and declamations, and to provide them the opportunity to express their personal response to her work. (Additional poems should be photocopied and presented to students, both in oral and written form.)

Word Choice and Imagery [Exercise sheet ☐]

Our purpose here is to encourage students to exercise an adventurous (perhaps out-of-character) attitude toward word choice and to discover the interesting imagery (and concepts) that can often thereby be created.

From *Great Stories Behind Famous Books.* Copyright © 1999 by Don L. Wulffson. (Alleyside Press, 1999)

Creative Writing [Exercise sheet ☐]

The previous activity can be a springboard into the writing of poetry, or students can approach this poetry-writing experience in any manner they choose. Encourage them to be open-minded; promote an atmosphere—and attitude—in which they are neither intimated by the assignment nor self-conscious about their work.

Library and Information-Seeking Skills

[Exercise sheet ☐]

1. The *Microsoft Encarta Encyclopedia* or any other print or electronic encyclopedia will provide comparative information on the authors.

2. The *AMA* or any other medical dictionary should provide a description of agoraphobia, but students may need to use a variety of search terms to locate specific examples of eccentric or reclusive behavior in more general tools.

3. An early edition of *Bartlett's Familiar Quotations* is available on the Internet if the school or public library does not have a copy.

Chapter 10

To Look Death in the Eye

Dostoyevsky

Early morning, December 22, 1849. St. Petersburg, Russia—the Peter and Paul Fortress, one of the most horrid and dreaded prisons of the time.

In filthy prison garb, his feet wrapped in rags, a thin blanket over his shoulders, Feodor paced. Echoing down the gloomy hallway, from other cells came the screams, imprecations, and wailings of other condemned men. Feodor tried to press his ears closed to the sound of it; it was impossible. He wanted to scream, too, and to cry out against his fate; it would do no good, though, he knew. He wanted to pray, but could not: his present predicament, and before that his exposure to the tenets of nihilism and atheism, had caused him to waver in the Christian faith of his boyhood. All was useless, pointless; soon he would be dead, and there was no way to change that numbing reality. His life was beyond rescue, his soul beyond redemption.

Through the single window of his cell, fanged with long, dirty icicles, a piercing, frigid wind blew. From it, gazing into the distance, Feodor could see a crowd beginning to gather near the gallows where he would die. But he would not be hung; the ropes were frozen. Instead, within the hour, he would be shot; his life of 27 years would come to an end.

For what?

He had written about social injustice in his country, Czarist Russia. And he had spoken out about it; in public, he had taken the podium to demand freedom from censorship, reform in the courts, and the abolition of serfdom—of the enslavement, really, of the Russian people by its monarchist, dictatorial government.

That was his "crime;" death was his punishment, and that which is worse than death—to await it, to know its nearness, to feel its relentless approach, like the increasingly heavy pounding of one's own heart.

And then there were his comrades, his friends. Fourteen in all, they too had been pulled from their beds in the middle of the night by soldiers; arrested, taken to jail, and from there led in chains to a sham trial where the verdict had already been decided. His friends. For the same crime—for remonstrating against the government—they too were living out the last few moments of their lives. In the same prison, in their own cells, like Feodor, they awaited death.

A rattling of iron keys. The squealing of rusty hinges. Heavy footfalls. And then the bang of iron doors. The guards were coming for him.

"It's time," said one of them, a torch in hand.

Feodor could only nod.

In his rag-wrapped feet, guards leading the way, soldiers behind him, he shuffled down a long corridor, light from the torch dancing on walls, briefly illuminating other wretches in their cells, who dolefully and silently watched the passing of the condemned man. For a moment the macabre cortege stopped, then continued on—now down a winding stairwell and then along another corridor, barred gates opening at their approach, closing behind them with horrid finality. And yet another door—but this one led outside. A blast of freezing cold air greeted Feodor; and he blinked at the feeble brightness of the early-morning sun.

"Move!" The barrel of a soldier's rifle rammed him in the back.

Snow crunching beneath his feet, rounding a corner with his guards, Feodor beheld a sight which both gladdened and horrified him: his friends. They were getting aboard horse-drawn carts. Like him, all would soon be in their graves; still, his last moments on earth would be spent with his friends.

Quiet greetings were exchanged, as were brave words, shared words of encouragement. The cart began to move, and silence settled over the condemned men as each surrendered to the ghastly, all-consuming fear of the reality of what awaited them.

Too quickly, the journey was coming to an end; they were approaching the gallows Feodor had seen from his cell. The wooden platform was now draped in black and guarded by soldiers. The once small crowd had grown to thousands—men, women, and children waiting quietly, all eyes on the condemned men. Now and again, instinctively, a glance would drift in another direction—to a cart bearing fourteen coffins. And then to a firing squad.

One of the prisoners began to weep.

Feodor put an arm about his shoulders. "Best to get it over with," he managed to say, fighting back his own terror.

"The lot of you! Down with you!" barked a soldier.

A moment later they were standing together in freshly fallen snow. Nervously, a young priest began to preach to them on the "wages of sin." His voice trembled as he closed with, "and may God have mercy on your souls."

When the priest had finished, the condemned men were made to remove their outer clothing and then to put on hooded white linen smocks—their burial shrouds.

The first three prisoners were ordered forward, and each led to a separate post. Feodor, next in line, watched as they were bound to the posts; a last prayer was said for them by the priest as their hoods were pulled over their faces. The firing squad moved into position; rifles were checked. And then the order was given:

Ready!.......... Aim!..........

At that moment, a messenger on horseback galloped onto the scene, a document in hand. The czar had commuted the sentences! Instead of death, the prisoners were to be sentenced to varying terms of hard labor.

A roar of approval went up from the crowd. Openly, the prisoners wept. Feodor dropped to his knees, numb with shock, his heart still racing, his mind and soul still reeling from the stupefying sequence of events. "I am saved!" he mumbled over and over, then clasped his hands together and gazed upward. "Thank you, God!" he cried.

Later, the young man would become a writer. Profoundly impacted by his horrifying, near-death experience, he would write of the "wages of sin," of wrong-doing and its consequences, of tragedy and suffering, of looking death in the eye, and at that moment, finding salvation—deliverance of body and soul through the intervention of a higher power. In due course, Feodor—Feodor Dostoyevsky—would be heralded as one of the world's greatest writers for his stories and novels, for *Crime and Punishment, The Idiot, The Devils, Notes From Underground,* and *The Brothers Karamazov.*

A footnote: When Feodor Dostoyevsky died at the age of 60, it is unlikely that he was aware of what had actually happened on the day of his execution—on the day in which his life was forever changed. The czar had never intended to have the prisoners shot. The preparations for the execution and the last-minute reprieve had all been staged; a sham, a wickedly shrewd demonstration of the power of the czar as well as his goodness and mercy—that is what the whole episode had been.

From *Great Stories Behind Famous Books.* Copyright © 1999 by Don L. Wulffson. (Alleyside Press, 1999)

Student Assignment

Before Reading Activity

Imagine that you have exactly fifteen minutes left to live. On a piece of paper, write the following:

1. The one thing for which you would most want to be remembered

2. That which you most regret having done in your life

3. That which you most regret not having done

4. A farewell note to the person you care about most

Critical Thinking

1. What was the ultimate irony of Dostoyevsky's "execution"?

2. Were the people in the crowd at the execution sympathetic to the beliefs and plight of the condemned men? If so, how do you know this?

3. An author's tone is his attitude toward his subject matter. For example, the author may be sarcastic, angry, sympathetic, light-hearted, etc., in the tone he adopts. How would you describe the author's tone in "To Look Death in the Eye?" Would the word "empathetic" be one of the words you might use here?

4. The mood of a piece of writing is how it affects the reader, how it makes him feel. What, for you, was the mood of the selection?

5. In what ways, if any, does the selection read like a work of fiction? In what ways is it unlike a work of fiction?

6. In what ways was Dostoyevsky changed, impacted, by his traumatic experience? Some of these changes are suggested in "To Look Death in the Eye." By conjecture, can you think other ways in which he may have been affected, both on a short-term and long-term basis?

7. It has been said that great writing is often born of great suffering. In what ways, and to what extent, does this hold true of Dostoyevsky—and of other writers you have studied in this book?

8. What similarities, if any, do you see between the beliefs of Steinbeck and those of Dostoyevsky?

Punctuation

Following each sentence are the punctuation marks needed to write that sentence. Rewrite each sentence, putting the marks where you believe they belong.

1. You should go to the police suggested the friend
   , " . "

2. A foul deep pond near where the car had been found was dredged without success   . — ,

3. No trace of the woman had been found she had vanished   . ;

4. Her husband would be arrested tried for murder found guilty and hung   , . , ,

5. And then there was the cars ignition it was off proving that the car had been pushed into the pit not driven   , . ' — ,

6. Were you at the party all evening asked the inspector   " . ? " ,

From Great Stories Behind Famous Books. Copyright © 1999 by Don L. Wulffson. (Alleyside Press, 1999)

7. And the police guessed indeed they were sure they had a case of murder on their hands   , — — .

8. A few days after the conversation on a frigid icy night in December 1926 a car was found
   . , , , ,

9. Unless of course she had no need of it unless as was apparently the case she was dead   , , , — !

10. Until 1926 Ms Christie had had considerable success as a mystery writer but then came her strange and devilishly clever albeit failed attempt at real life murder   ; . , ( )

The answers to the above can be found in the selection "To Stir a Mysterious Mind."

Understanding Conflict

Conflict—struggles between opposing forces—are to be found in all fictional works and most nonfiction. For example, imagine a story about a man in love with a woman he later finds out wants to kill him. You want to know how this conflict ends—and that is what keeps you turning the pages.

There are seven basic types of conflict.

People Against People — An example would be a story about a boy tormented by the school bully.

People Against Nature — An example would be a young girl lost in a forest on a freezing night.

People Against Society — An example would be a story about a person working to change laws that are unfair to elderly people.

People Against Machinery and Science — An example would be a computer that learns to think on its own and tries to destroy its inventor.

People at Odds with Themselves (mental conflict) — An example would be a man who commits a crime for which his best friend is accused.

People Against the Supernatural — An example would be girl who can tell how, when, and where people will die by just looking at them.

People Against the Unknown — An example would be colonists who are sent to a planet—one where all of the previous colonists died mysteriously.

For each of the following stories, describe the central conflict(s). (*Master Plots* and the synopses in "Recommended for Further Reading" will be of help to you in some instances for this activity.)

1. *A Night to Remember*

2. *Of Mice and Men*

3. *Robinson Crusoe*

4. *Dracula*

5. *Dr. Jekyll & Mr. Hyde*

6. *Frankenstein*

7. "To Look Death in the Eye"

Creative Writing

Write a story which utilizes one of the above types of conflict as its central source of momentum. If you wish, use one of the example story lines.

Library and Information-Seeking Skills

1. Define nihilism, atheism, conversion, and salvation. How do these relate to the story of Feodor Dostoyevsky in this entry?

2. Research the conditions of the populace in Czarist Russia at the time of Dostoyevsky in the mid-1800s. Was his treatment unusual? What powers did the Czar have? When did the last Czar reign and how did his reign end?

3. Research a later Russian writer, Aleksandr Solzhenitsyn. In what ways are his life and writings similar or dissimilar to those of Dostoyevsky?

From *Great Stories Behind Famous Books*. Copyright © 1999 by Don L. Wulffson. (Alleyside Press, 1999)

Teacher Resources
Whole Language Activities for "To Look Death in the Eye"

Before Reading Activity [Exercise sheet ☐]

The goal of the activity is to prepare the students for the reading selection by asking them to empathize with the thoughts and feelings of someone who was condemned to die.

During Reading Activity

1. As homework, have students read the selection into a tape-recorder. After previewing these, play one or more of the best readings to the class.

2. Have students read the selection silently.

After Reading Activities

Critical Thinking [Exercise sheet ☐]

Among the many specific goals of this activity are:

1. Increasing students understand of the selection, including the use of inferential and conjectural thinking;

2. Acquainting students with the terms "tone" and "mood;"

3. Having students compare and contrast the lives, belief-systems, and writings of the various authors considered in this book.

Punctuation [Exercise sheet ☐]

The goal of the material is to familiarize students with some fairly sophisticated punctuation usage. Have students correct the work on their own. Put the assignment on an overhead projector, and then go over it with them orally, quickly pointing out some of the applicable rules.

Understanding Conflict [Exercise sheet ☐]

The activity familiarizes the students with some of the basics of conflict, which they may then apply to works they have read in the past and those they will encounter in the future.

Creative Writing [Exercise sheet ☐]

An understanding and appreciation of conflict is an essential resource in writing creatively. Thus, in addition to developing their personal potential for creative writing, the activity provides students with a vehicle for starting and continuing to fulfill their creative work.

Library and Information-Seeking Skills

[Exercise sheet ☐]

1. Any unabridged dictionary can be used to answer this question.

2. A history of Russia prior to the Soviet Revolution would be the best source of information on life in Czarist Russia. However, some encyclopedias may provide general background and references to more extensive works.

3. *The Reader's Advisor* will provide a list of additional Russian authors, and these can be researched using either the library catalog or the name-search capability of a Web search engine.

Chapter 11

To Stir a Curious Mind

Agatha Christie

This is a true story—one of infidelity, intrigue, and murder.

A man was seeing another woman, cheating on his wife. And his wife found out; bit by bit, she came upon the evidence, and her heart was broken. Just to make sure, she did a bit of detective work. She spied on her husband—and found not only that it was true, but that he was planning on leaving her. Afterward, he planned to divorce her and marry the other woman. At first, she considered confronting him, and pleading with him to stay with her. But then she changed her mind, and decided to kill him.

The perfect crime—that is what the anguished but brilliant woman planned. She would make it seem as though her husband had murdered *her*. The police and the courts would do the rest. Her husband would be arrested, tried, found guilty, and hung.

"I think my husband is cheating on me," she told a friend one day. "I think he wants to do away with me, and marry this other woman."

"You should go to the police," suggested the friend.

"But I have no proof." She dabbed at her eyes. "Besides, I'm probably just letting my imagination get the best of me. Surely, he wouldn't kill me!"

But then it happened. A few days after the conversation, on a frigid, icy night in December 1926, a car was found *her* car—at the bottom of a cliff, concealed in a pit. Signs of foul play were everywhere. No trace of the woman could be found; she had vanished. And then there was the car's ignition—it was off, proving that the car had been pushed into the pit, not driven. And last but not least, in the vehicle was the woman's expensive coat. Why, on a freezing, cold night would she not wear her coat? Unless, of course, she had no need of it—unless, as was apparently the case, she was dead!

A large search party was organized. Every inch of a 40-square-mile area in the vicinity of the car was canvassed—in search of clues … and the body. Tracking dogs were brought in; light planes crisscrossed the immediate area, and beyond. A foul, deep pond near where the car had been found was dredged—without success.

The days passed, and there was no sign of the woman. The police guessed—indeed, they were sure—they had a case of murder on their hands. And who, naturally, was the first and most logical suspect?

The woman's husband was hauled in for interrogation.

"Where were you on the night in question?" demanded the inspector.

The man hemmed and hawed. His face turned red. He was embarrassed; though a married man, he had, he said, been with another woman—at a party. They were going to get married; and, in fact, had planned on announcing this at the party.

"Were you at the party all evening?" asked the inspector.

"No," he admitted. "You see, I received a phone call from my wife. She was angry, furious, in tears. She had found out what was going on, and said she was going to come to the party to make a scene."

"And what did you do when she threatened this?" the policeman demanded to know.

"I left the party," the husband admitted, head hanging. "I went home to calm her down."

The inspector sneered. "Instead, there was a fight," he surmised. "You killed her, hid the car, then got rid of the body!"

"No," pleaded the man. "No, no one was home, and so I just returned to the party."

The inspector laughed at the lame story. The man was arrested for murder. And a trial was scheduled.

The story was in all the papers, complete with photos of the missing—and presumed murdered—woman. However, because of the photographs, the carefully laid plot unraveled. An anonymous letter tipped off police that the woman was living in a small hotel on the other side of England. When police found her, she feigned amnesia. When asked if she had any idea of who she was, she smiled, and gave the name of the woman her husband had been seeing.

But the police knew better. They knew they had found the lady they had long believed had been murdered—someone named Agatha Christie.

Until 1926, Ms. Christie had some success as a mystery writer; but then came her strange and devilishly clever (albeit failed) attempt at a real-life murder. Her already vivid imagination was given a powerful shove by reality; it blossomed, her talent flourished, and was brought fully to life by her first-hand, real-life brush with the world of mystery.

To date, Agatha Christie has published eighty mysteries; 300 million copies of her works have been sold; next to Shakespeare, she is the second most-translated English author. When asked about her strange disappearance, she still claims no memory of it—then smiles. Asked if the incident somehow served to foment—and shape her enormously successful career, she denies it completely. After all, she suffers from complete amnesia, she says. How could something affect her that she does not remember—at all?

Oh, by the way, the real name of this masterful mystery writer is Agatha Miller. For some strange reason she writes under the name of someone from her forgotten past—a husband who cheated on her, and almost lost his life because of it. Perhaps it is just coincidence, but his last name was Christie.

Student Assignment

Comparative Thinking

1. What similarities (and differences) do you see between how *Frankenstein* and *Dr. Jekyll & Mr. Hyde* came to be?

2. What similarities do you see between the origins of *Robinson Crusoe, Dr. Jekyll & Mr. Hyde, Dracula* and *A Night to Remember*?

   What differences do you see?

3. Do you see a similarity in how Steinbeck's works and those of the Bronte sisters came to be?

4. Describe some of the sad occurrences in the lives of the authors.

5. With which of the authors do you identify most? Why?

6. Of all the works mentioned, which would you be proudest of having written? Why?

7. Of all the selections in this book, which did you enjoy most? Which did you enjoy least? Explain your answer.

Word-Skills Development (Cooperative)

Write a word-skills development activity for another student to complete. The activity may:

1. Deal with any area of language (e.g.: spelling, etymology)

2. Deal with words in the present selection, past selections, or consist of random words

3. It may be in the form of a puzzle, game, or ordinary classwork

Exchange activities with another student; write:

Answered by __(your name)_____

at the bottom of the paper.

Have the other student correct your work and turn it in to the teacher.

Creative Thinking and Writing

A: Fill in the blanks with words that would create a mystery. Try to think of *unusual* things. For example: A girl finds photographs of herself at a place she has never been.

1. A _____ in a wheelchair receives a(n) _____, and the next day _____ is found dead. A detective finds _____ _____ and several _____ hidden in _____.

2. In an attic _____ finds a suitcase in which there is (are) _____. Nearby are several _____. The strange thing about them is that _____ _____.

3. Chris reads in the papers that _____ has been kidnapped. But that day _____ _____. Later, _____ Chris finds _____ scattered all over the floor of _____.

At the police station, a woman suddenly yells that _____. Startling Chris, the police _____

4. While hiking, two _____ are shocked when they find a car in which _____ _____. They lead the police back to the spot, but strangely _____. Suddenly _____.

5. Pat paints a picture of _____. Later, Pat sees _____. Returning home, Pat finds that the picture _____. Then Pat hears_____.

B: Write a mystery story or play based on one of the above scenarios.

Or

Write an essay in which you compare and contrast the manner in which various literary works came to be. You may consider all the selections in this book, several selections, or just two. (The smaller the number of selections dealt with, the more thorough and in-depth the essay should be.)

Library and Information-Seeking Skills

1. What was unusual about the book *The Murder of Roger Ackroyd* by Agatha Christie? Use a history of mystery writing or information about Christie's writing to find the information. As an alternative, find two or three interesting facts about any of Christie's other books.

2. Make a filmography of movies made from Agatha Christie's books. Use three or more sources, such as websites on Christie or films, *Contemporary Authors*, or books about Christie, to make sure your filmography is complete. Make your filmography in date order, by year, followed by titles.

3. Using resources on mystery writing or on Agatha Christie, find the names of three of Christie's most famous detectives. Research them further and write a brief paragraph about each, including a physical description and other special characteristics.

Teacher Resources
Whole Language Activities for "To Stir a Curious Mind"

Before Reading Activity

Show a movie or video of an Agatha Christie classic. (Recommended: *Murder on the Orient Express; Death on the Nile;* or *Witness for the Prosecution.*). As the students watch the movie, have them select three of the five following questions:

a)   A factual question;

b)   A question regarding fact versus opinion;

c)   A question regarding inference;

d)   A question regarding characterization;

e)   A question requiring analysis, evaluation, and critical thinking.

Have them ask the class at least one question. Have all students write a summary of the movie.

During Reading Activity

1.   Have the students read the selection silently.

2.   Tell students to write down three questions.

   a)   A factual question

   b)   A question concerning fact versus opinion

   c)   A question requiring analysis and critical thinking

3.   Have them ask the class at least one of their questions.

After Reading Activities

Cooperative Learning

The activity promotes the growth of listening and social-interaction skills, both cooperative and competitive. Moreover, it serves to test and to reinforce students' retention of basic details from the reading selections in chapters 1 through 11. To assist those who have used the readings selectively, the chapter from which each question was drawn is given in parentheses along with the answer.

Note: If desired, prior to the activity, students can be told to review the reading selections as homework. Too, the test can be given on an individual basis or an open-book basis.

1.   Collect the reading selection, and have them clear their desks.

2.   Divide the class into three or four teams, identifying them as Team 1, Team 2, Team 3, Team 4; appoint a leader for each team.

3.   Have students number from 1 to 15 on their papers.

4.   Say: "I am going to ask 30 questions about selections you have read in this book. The team that has the most correct answers will get an "A," that with the second most will get a "B," and so on." (Or use any technique consistent with your own grading system.)

5.   Ask the first question of Team 1. Give team members time to discuss possible answers, then have the team's spokesperson give the answer the team has decided on. If the answer is correct, a point is scored; if incorrect, ask Team 2 the same question. Continue asking the same question until it is answered correctly. If not answered correctly after asked of all teams, present the question again to the teams, each time giving a clue.

6.   Ask the next question of the team that numerically follows the team that answered the previous question correctly. (For example, if Team 2 got the right answer to the first question, then Team 3 gets first shot at the second question.)

7.   Have all students take notes on the questions and answers.

Questions

1. What was the occupation of the father of the Bronte sisters? (minister, chapter 5)

2. Which of the sisters wrote *Jane Eyre*? (Charlotte, chapter 5)

3. In what city did Branwell go to college? (London, chapter 5)

4. What was the name of the college? (Royal Academy of the Arts, chapter 5)

5. In what illegal drug did Branwell indulge? (opium, chapter 5)

6. What was the last name of the pseudonym (pen name) the sisters used? (Bell, chapter 5)

7. What does the name Dracula mean? (son of the devil, chapter 4)

8. In 1883 a law was passed in England to prevent people from doing what? (driving stakes through the hearts of those who'd committed suicide, chapter 4)

9. What did Vlad Tepes do to the Turkish ambassadors? (nailed their turbans to their heads, chapter 4)

10. Of what was Elizabeth Bathory most afraid? (getting old, chapter 4)

11. What was the original title of *Alice in Wonderland*? (*Alice's Adventures Underground*, chapter 3)

12. How were two of Alice Hargreaves sons killed? (in WWI, chapter 3)

13. How long did it take R.L. Stevenson to write *Dr. Jekyll & Mr. Hyde?* (3 days, chapter 2)

14. Why did one of William Brodie's own gang turn him in? (he abandoned them during a robbery attempt, chapter 2)

15. How long was Alexander Selkirk stranded on the island? (more than four years, chapter 1)

16. Where did Selkirk dig a cave in Scotland? (on his family's property, chapter 1)

17. What is the full name of the island on which Selkirk was stranded? (Juan Fernandez, chapter 1)

18. Why was Daniel Defoe put in jail? (for his writings which attacked the government, chapter 1)

19. How many pencils did John Steinbeck sharpen each morning? (24, chapter 8)

20. What university did Steinbeck attend? (Stanford, chapter 8)

21. What was the original title of *Of Mice and Men?* (*Something That Happened*, chapter 8)

22. In what state did Emily Dickinson live? (Massachusetts, chapter 9)

23. Fill in the blank. "How dreary to be somebody/How public like a _____. (frog, chapter 8)

24. How many of Emily Dickinson's poems were published during her lifetime? (seven, chapter 8)

25. For what "crime" was Dostoyevsky sentenced to death? (writing/speaking against social injustice, chapter 10)

26. What color was the hooded garment (smock) that Dostoyevsky and the other condemned men were made to wear? (white, chapter 10)

27. In what year did Agatha Christie disappear? (1926, chapter 11)

28. Why did the police believe Ms. Christie's car had been pushed into the pit? (the ignition was off, chapter 11)

29. How did Ms. Christie get her husband to leave the party? (called and threatened to cause a scene, chapter 11)

30. Whose name did Agatha Christie give as being her own when she was found by police? (that of the woman her husband had been seeing, chapter 11)

Comparative Thinking [Exercise sheet ☐]

It is important that students see the similarities and differences in the geneses of the various works considered in the book. Also, ask them to look for other similarities and differences (and bases of comparison) not dealt with in the questions.

Answers:

1. What similarities (and differences) do you see between how *Frankenstein* and *Dr. Jekyll & Mr. Hyde* came to be? (In a dream *Frankenstein* was the consequence of a contest.)

2. What similarities do you see between the origins of *Robinson Crusoe, Dr. Jekyll & Mr. Hyde, Dracula* and *A Night to Remember*? (Based on true events and real people.)

   What differences do you see? (The last is non-fiction.)

3. Do you see a similarity in how Steinbeck's works and those of the Bronte sisters came to be? (All wrote about the people, the places, and the life they knew.)

4. Describe some of the sad occurrences in the lives of the authors. (The Bronte sisters led rather desolate lives and were treated like second-class citizens; Carroll was rejected in his marriage proposal; Morgan Robertson, tormented by parallels of his book to the *Titanic,* died an alcoholic.)

   Questions 5–7 all ask for students' opinions.

Word-Skills Development (Cooperative)

[Exercise sheet ☐]

The student is once again made an active participant in the whole of the language-arts learning process. Suggest the following as possible areas in which to develop activities: homophones; multiple meanings for one word; hyperbole; affixes; synonyms; word choice; silent letters; parts of speech; plurals; comparatives and superlatives, etc. One suggestion might be a crossword puzzle—and possibly one with a new twist: instead of definitions, etymologies are given. Some of the better activities can be photocopied and done by the class; or, perhaps a compilation of activities by several different students can be prepared and assigned.

Creative Thinking and Writing [Exercise sheet ☐]

Prepare an overhead of the assignment. With the class, discuss/write down different words/phrases that could be put in a specific blank. Too, discuss/write down responses to whole story lines (whole paragraphs). Students may work in pairs or teams in writing the story, as well as individually. Have the students read and comment upon each others' stories. With the class, write a play on an overhead projector. Have the students offer suggestions as you write and also copy down the play. When it is finished, the play can either be read aloud, or it can be acted out on videotape and shown to the class.

Library and Information-Seeking Skills

[Exercise sheet ☐]

1. Use this question to encourage students to search both in the library catalog and the Web for information about Agatha Christie and *The Murder of Roger Ackroyd.*

2. *Contemporary Authors* is a good print source of information, but students could be directed to use a Web browser such as Yahoo if a copy of this resource is not readily available in the library.

3. *The Reader's Advisor* or any other guide to mysteries can be used to answer this question.

Chapter 12

Diagnosis: Innocent

Doyle

A lovely setting for a murder …

Glasgow, Scotland—1908. A frigid December night, the city wet with fog, blackly glistening with the stuff. A girl, fourteen years old, moves through it, down the street. But she is only a head; the fog—it has settled low to the ground, rendering her body invisible as she passes the affluent Queen's Terraces apartment building.

Suddenly, from an upstairs room comes a piercing scream, followed by the sounds of a violent scuffle—a table going over, a lamp and glassware breaking, then something thrown, and hitting with a loud bang.

The girl in the street is gazing upward, at the apartment. As is an old man—from the window of his home, across the street. And a maid is running up a flight of stairs that leads to the apartment of Miss Marion Gilchrist.

Another scream, and then the horrid sound of the impact of a heavy object with flesh … and a moment later the door of Miss Gilchrist's apartment flies open. The maid is knocked sprawling as a man rushes down the stairs; wide-eyed, the fourteen-year-old girl stares, numb with shock, as he races right past her; and from across the street the old man who is peering out the window glimpses the fleeing figure … until it is swallowed up by the fog.

Graying hair red with blood. Skull crushed. Eyes blank, transfixed. Marion Gilchrist lies dead in the shambles of the front room of her apartment as the police interrogate the maid, the teenage girl, and the elderly man who had been watching from his window.

The motive, according to police: robbery.

Detectives discover a diamond brooch has been taken. The next day it turns up—in a local pawnshop.

"Bloke by the name o' Slater brung it," the pawnbroker says. "Oscar Slater—a German immigrant. Owns a gamblin' club."

Slater is brought in for questioning.

"I do not do this thing," he protests in halting, German-accented English. Struggling for words, he assures the police they have the wrong man, and tries to explain about the brooch. "I not do nothing," he says. "This you will see."

But to his disbelief, all three witnesses identify him as the killer. At his trial, Slater pleads his innocence—fumbling for words, trying hard to make himself understood.

The trial is quick. The verdict: guilty. The sentence: life in prison.

Nineteen years pass—slowly. Slater languishes in his cell, still protesting his innocence. His English improves—greatly. He learns to speak clearly, to write well, and to read. Reading—it becomes one of his true pleasures. And, as we all do, he has his favorite author.

Slater's favorite is a medical doctor, an interesting man who, over the years, had come to look upon all medical cases as detective work. In time, the doctor tried his hand at writing—and with his sleuth-like perspective on medicine, not surprisingly, he wrote detective stories—with such success that he eventually all but abandoned the profession for which he had been trained.

Sitting in his cell, an unusual notion strikes Slater.

Taking pen in hand, he writes a lengthy letter to the doctor-turned-writer. In great detail, he describes the crime for which he is sentenced to a life behind bars, explains that he has no one else to turn to, and begs the author to re-examine the evidence.

Receiving the letter, the author is intrigued—both by the prisoner's story and by the unusual circumstances of the man's request for help. After all, he is a writer of mysteries, of detective fiction—not a lawyer or private investigator.

Not entirely sure of how to proceed, he nevertheless begins to look into the case.

First, he interviews the two eyewitnesses who are still alive, the maid and teenager (now a 33-year-old woman). "The police put pressure on us to finger Slater," both admit. And no, they were not then—and are not now—sure it had been Slater they had seen on the night of the murder.

More digging. Only the brooch had been stolen ... yet there had been $12,000 worth of jewelry in Ms. Gilchrist's apartment. In addition, the woman had written a will just prior to her murder that had also disappeared. Had robbery really been the motive? If so, then why had only the one piece of jewelry been taken? And what had happened to the will?

With a keen eye, the author reads the transcripts from the trial—over and over. The paper is yellowing, old. Still, it is all there: glaringly, many of the trial judge's comments are blatantly prejudicial. Repeatedly, remarks made by him convey wholesale certitude of Slater's guilt. Too, there is clear bias—outright animosity—against people of German ancestry.

And then there is the issue of Mr. Slater's difficulty with English. The transcripts are a clear demonstration of a man unable to put his thoughts—his defense—into words. Garbled. His explanation—his attempted elucidation of the critical details of how and why he had the brooch in hand—is barely intelligible. Still, it is clear enough ...

Slater had won it at the small gambling club he had owned.

For the author, proving this contention is vital—but it seems almost impossible, for the event happened almost two decades ago. Weeks pass. The writer thinks long and hard—and has a sudden inspiration: the shop where the brooch had been pawned. Moldering records—he tackles them, endlessly pores over them. And suddenly, there it is before him. In black-and-write, it is written: The brooch, the key to the whole case, had been pawned by Slater weeks before the murder of Marion Gilchrist!

Now positive of the man's innocence, the mystery writer petitions members of Parliament. A hearing is held. Concisely, expertly, impressively, he presents the evidence he has gathered. And Oscar Slater is set free.

Sobbing, he grips the hand of his savior.

Of Arthur Conan Doyle—the masterful creator of Sherlock Holmes.

Student Assignment

Cause and Effect

In reading, as in real life, we see many cause-and-effect relationships. Simply speaking, this means that for anything that happens (effect) there is a cause. Match the causes with their effects given below. (Match the numbers and letters.)

Cause

1. The sounds of a violent scuffle could be heard.

2. The maid was running up the stairs.

3. Slater's English skills improved greatly while in prison.

4. Doyle's stories were a success.

5. Slater was a recent immigrant to England.

6. Doyle's writing showed an aptitude for analytical thinking—and detective work.

7. Slater spoke English poorly.

8. Doyle was intrigued by Slater's letter.

9. The police did not know Slater had pawned the brooch before the murder.

Effect

A. He spoke English poorly and with a strong accent.

B. Slater believed the man could prove his innocence.

C. The teenager looked up at the apartment.

D. He was able to leave his medical practice.

E. He was able to explain himself clearly to Doyle, and at his second trial.

F. He decided to get involved in the case.

G. She got knocked down by the fleeing murderer.

H. He could not explain himself well at the trial.

I. A critical bit of information was not brought forward at his trial.

Evaluative and Comparative Thinking

1. The climax of a work comes when the reader's questions are answered. In "Diagnosis: Innocent," there are two primary questions. The first is whether Slater will finally be released from jail; and, climactically, we find that he is. What is the other question you asked yourself as you read the story? What was the answer?

2. Explain the title in relation to the incidents and characters in the story.

3. Not until the last part of "Diagnosis: Innocent" do you learn the identity of the author in question. In what other selections in this book is this technique used? Too, why do you think the author chose to employ it on numerous occasions?

4. Generally speaking, the setting of a work is the time and place in which it occurs. What is the setting of this selection?

5. As this true story begins, what are some of the specifics of the setting? (And what are some of the words, phrases, and images used to create this setting?)

6. As the story opens, what sort of effect does the setting have upon the mood of the work—that is, upon the way you, as the reader, feel?

Technique and Tense

Most other selections in this book are written in past tense, while "Diagnosis: Innocent" is written in present tense. First, redo the selection so that it is written in its entirety in past tense, as follows:

A girl, fourteen years old, moves _____ through it, down the street. But she is _____ only a head; the fog—it has _____ settled low to the ground, rendering her body invisible as she passes _____ the affluent Queen's Terraces apartment building…

What differences are there in "Diagnosis: Innocent" in present as opposed to past tense? Do you prefer it in present tense or past tense—and why? What, if any, reasons can you see for "Diagnosis: Innocent" having originally been written in present tense?

Plot

1. The plot of a story is its basic sequence of events. The events of the following story are in the wrong order. Correct this by numbering the events in the order in which they belong.

a) ___ All of the sculptures are of mythological figures—Venus, Hercules. Poseidon.

b) ___ Their first week in the new town they learn that, over the years, three people in Benville have disappeared—a beautiful woman, a very strong man, and an old fisherman.

c) ___ A month later, the brother and sister take house-cleaning jobs at the home of an eccentric artist named E.G. Dadama, who has many lifelike, bronze works of sculpture.

d) ___ A few weeks after the mother disappears, there is a new sculpture in Dadama's study—that of an Amazonian woman.

e) ___ Shondra and Cody do a bit of detective work and discover that the missing people are inside the bronze "mythological" statues. The beautiful woman is the Venus statue; the strong man is in the statue of Hercules; the old fisherman is in the Poseidon statue; and Dadama's mother is in the huge bronze statue of the Amazonian woman.

f) ___ Shondra and Cody move with their dad to Benville, Alabama.

g) ___ After working there for some time, Dadama's mother, a huge, Amazonian woman, disappears.

2. The climax of a story is the "moment of truth," that is, it is that moment when the conflicts are resolved and the truth of what has been going on is revealed. Of the above items, which is the climax of the story?

Writing

Write a detective story based on the preceding plot—or on a plot of your own device.

Or, read one of Doyle's mysteries featuring Sherlock Holmes. First, write a critical essay on the story. Secondly, create an activity like the "plot" exercise above—with the events in the wrong order. Photocopy the activity for your classmates to do.

Just for Fun: A Cryptogrammatical Story

In cryptogram puzzles, the letters in the words have been replaced with other letters. For example, the sentence *He went home* might be written as *CR XRLG CTVR.* Notice how the words are in their right order with a space after each. Also, each letter substitution remains the same throughout.

The following "true detective" story is in the form

of a cryptogram. Break the code and figure out the story. Keep the following in mind:

1. One-letter words are A or I.

2) The word *the* occurs very frequently in the English language, as do *and, is, it,* and *of.*

And here's a clue that will get you off to a good, sleuthful start: The title of the story is *Bungler.*

LXPAQMU

C LXUAQCU VPSM LUVBM RPFV CP VKKRSM. YM JFVQM C JZCQQ SVZEXFMU, C FCEM UMSVUIMU, CP CIIRPA ZCSYRPM, CPI JMOMUCQ VFYMU RFMZJ.

FYM LXUAQCU ZCIM VPM QRFFQM ZRJFCBM IXURPA FYM UVLLMUN YM IUVEEMI YRJ HCQQMF. FYM HCQQMF, HYRSY SVPFCRPMI C IUROMUJ QRSMPJM CPI VFYMU RIMPFRKRSCFRVP, HCJ KVXPI LN EVQRSM.

FYM EVQRSM RZZMIRCFMQN IUVOM FV FYM YVZM VK LVL PMQJVP. FYMN YCEERQN UMFXUPMI ZU. PMQJVP'J HCQQMF FV YRZ, FYMP CUUMJFMI YRZ KVU UVLLMUN.

Library and Information-Seeking Skills

1. How many novels, novellas, and short stories did Arthur Conan Doyle write? When was the first published? What was the last book published before his death and in what year? How many editions of his books are currently in print? (Try checking one of the online bookstores or your library's version of *Books in Print* online or in book form.) How many editions of Doyle's books does your library contain?

2. Check the Web for some of the information pages on Sherlock Holmes. Are the curved pipe and deerstalker hat in the stories, or are they from some of the film versions? If so, what actor first used these props? What about the phrase "Elementary, my dear Watson"—originally in the story or in film? Try the website:

http://watserv1.uwaterloo.ca/~credmond/sh.html (Sherlockian Holmepage)

or another website.

3. How many different film adaptations and versions are there of Sherlock Holmes stories? What actors of film and TV were famous for playing Sherlock Holmes? Are there any parodies or spoofs of Holmes that you can find? Try film resources or websites.

Teacher Resources
Whole Language Activities for "Diagnosis: Innocent"

Before Reading Activity

Show a video of a mystery or detective story, stopping it near the climax. Discuss what has previously been shown, and then have the students suggest possible endings (who-done-it?). Encourage them to discuss clues, and to think deductively. After showing the ending, again discuss clues and various details foreshadowing the ending and final solution.

During Reading Activity

1. Read "Diagnosis: Innocent" aloud to students. Leave out the last line, that which identifies Doyle as the writer/detective. When students express their dissatisfaction with the reading selection—ending in this way, ask them: Why are you dissatisfied? Why do you want to know who the writer/detective was? And, who do you think the writer is (and on what clues do you base your conclusion)?

2. Have the students read the selection silently.

After Reading Activities

Cause and Effect [Exercise sheet □]

The goal of the activity is to help students recognize cause-and-effect relationships in what they read—and in their everyday lives. Call on them to describe examples of cause-and-effect situations (anecdotes) in their own lives.

Answers: (1) C, (2) G, (3) E, (4) D, (5) H, (6) B, (7) H, (8) F, (9) I.

Evaluative and Comparative Thinking
[Exercise sheet □]

The specific goals of the questions include broadening the students' awareness of the utilization (and importance) of various literary techniques in nonfictional (as well as fictional) writing—setting, mood, suspense, climax.

Technique and Tense [Exercise sheet □]

Discuss the impact of tense (e.g., the immediacy and intimacy of present tense). Also point out the importance of consistency of tense, which can be demonstrated by reading a portion of the selection aloud and randomly shifting back and forth from present to past tense. As an additional activity, have students change one of the other selections (e.g., "A Person in Two") into present tense.

Plot [Exercise sheet □]

The goal is to inculcate in the students an awareness of plot structure. Such an awareness helps them to better understand fictional structuring; moreover, it facilitates the ability to summarize a work (both orally and in writing).

Answers: (a) 4, (b) 2, (c) 3, (d) 6, (e) 7, (f) 1, (g) 5.

Writing [Exercise sheet □]

The activity dealing with plot lends students a tool for structuring their own creative writing; additionally, it will assist them as they tackle those aspects of essay writing where summarization is needed. The second assignment, which requires students to present classmates with an out-of-order plot, actively involves them in the learning process (which, when fully embraced, also includes participation in the teaching process).

Just for Fun: A Cryptogrammatical Story
[Exercise sheet □]

The reading selection and following activities provide natural segue into this puzzle, the primary goal of which is to reinforce the students' conviction that learning is fun.

Library and Information-Seeking Skills

[Exercise sheet ☐]

1. Use this question to encourage students to learn more about *Books in Print* and the numerous online bookstores such as Amazon.com.

2. If the referenced URL is no longer active, there is a wealth of information on Doyle and Sherlock Holmes available on other websites. Encourage the students to compare the quality of the various websites, and identify those they consider to be more accurate.

3. The best source of information to answer this question would be a film history encyclopedia. However, many of the more extensive websites include information on film adaptations.

The Man in the Black Velvet Mask

Dumas

The story…

Seventeenth-century France. The Bastille—the prison of all prisons. The stench of the place, redolent with the smell of urine, fecal matter, and decay—not only of things, but of men—the living dead, rotting in cells. Their screams and insane babblings; "But I am the king!" cries one … a new arrival, his voice mixing with the agonized calls of others, he is buffeted about by the jailer and guards as he stumblingly ascends the up-winding stairs of a tower. "But I am the …!" he begins to cry again— but then a gag is shoved in his mouth.

More stairs. More dark turns.

The jailer's keys rattle and a door opens onto the cell where he will be confined forever. Why? Because he IS the king! Or, rather the twin of the reigning king—and being the firstborn, he is the rightful heir to the throne of France!

To be locked for life in a small, stone-walled cell—the horror of it is beyond bearing. Yet there is an even greater horror to come…

A blacksmith and his assistant enter the place, the tools of their trade in hand … and something else, something concealed—veiled by a rag.

"Hold him!" orders the jailer.

The prisoner is thrown to the floor; a knee is planted on his chest and his arms and legs held. And then, as his eyes bulge in terror and disbelief, a mask of iron is clamped about his face—then welded shut.

Before they make their dark exits, his tormentors remove the gag from the prisoner's mouth; in a top-most cell of the Bastille, one far removed from the others, the prisoner may scream for eternity, as loudly as he likes.

No one will hear him.

Few will see him.

And those who do will not know his true identity, for no one will see the face of The Man In The Iron Mask.

The days pass …

At first the prisoner cries out. He beats his fist against the door and his iron-bound head against the wall … accomplishing nothing. He clasps his hands to the iron mask. He wails.

Days become weeks…the weeks become months …

The prisoner sits. He does nothing but lament the hideousness of his fate.

Months become years…

While upon the throne of France sits his twin— an arrogant, narcissistic, vile tyrant—under whose direction the bestial scheme has been accomplished. His cleverness! He relishes it—finds it amusing, pleasurable … as he does his debauchery and self-indulgence. His people, they suffer in squalor and poverty, mired in a hapless existence; but of what importance is that to him? And, as for his brother …

The prisoner. As the years pass, his clothing turns to rags. His skin filthy, raw. And within his mask, his own hair and beard grow, threatening to strangle him. If only they would. If only he could die, be released by death from The Mask—from a life without hope.

He has, of course, no way of knowing it, but there *is* hope; there are gallant men working—arduously, clandestinely—on his behalf—The Three Musketeers. After much planning, much scheming, and a plenitude of other adventures, they burst into the cell, release him from the dual bondage of the prison and the mask. And then, as it must be, he is enthroned, and replaces his twin brother as the King of France; but though a physical duplicate, morally—and in all other ways—he is his twin's opposite: caring, sensitive to the needs of his people, and generous. The nation of France now has the king it deserves—and has for so long needed.

Meanwhile …

It is predictable, of course; yet so ironically lovely, so necessary to the conclusion of the story—the situation for the twins is reversed. Thus, as it was before: Eyes bulging with horror, thrashing, the iron mask is closed forever about the head of a prisoner, the evil twin—as he shrieks, "But I am the king!"

And so ends Dumas' novel *The Man in the Iron Mask.*

An excellent tale.

But that is all it is, a work of fiction very loosely based upon an intriguing historical incident, one in which there is as little certitude as there is voluminous, relentless conjecture.

Only this is known for sure …

On Thursday, September 18, 1698, as the curious looked on, a heavily curtained litter was brought to the gates of the Bastille. From it stepped a man whose name was not spoken and whose face was covered with a mask of black velvet stiffened with whalebone. Under guard, the man strode forward, disappearing into the Bastille as the tower gate slammed closed behind him. Until his death, the mysterious individual remained in prison.

Whoever the man was, he was treated with courtesy, even deference. He was clothed and fed well; moreover, he was even allowed the privilege of having musical instruments in his cell, which he played hour after hour, year after year, to while away the time. Another strange fact—the prisoner seemed to accept his fate. Reports by his guards state that the man had "a sweet nature" and never complained. He never tried to remove his black velvet mask; instead, he seemed as determined as his captors always to keep his face hidden from view.

More than a century after the man's death, Alexander Dumas, the famous French author, of European-and-African descent, intrigued by this mysterious incident and personage, concocted a fascinating and enjoyable adventure story. Weaving fact with fiction, the author turned the cloth covering into a far more evocative substance—iron—and cast it in a far larger, more sinister shape, into a "metal helmet which enveloped the [entire] head."

Who the prisoner was and what crime—if any—he had committed are among the most haunting of historical mysteries, ones which, as mentioned, have fueled much speculation—the least credible and most debunked of the theories being that he was the twin brother of King Louis XIV, i.e., Dumas' story.

The Man in the Iron Mask is the final installment of Dumas' saga of chivalry and valor, which spans half a century of French history and runs to over a million and a quarter words. Scholars wince at the liberties he took; for in reality, whenever history failed to live up to his expectations, Dumas simply re-invented it, reworked it to satisfy his needs. This is evidenced not only in *The Iron Mask*, but in all his tales; perhaps most disappointing of all to readers is the fact that The Three Musketeers, though they existed, are primarily mythic products of a creative mind, their lives and exploits almost entirely fallacious. An examination of history reveals that there is nothing to suggest that they were in any way remarkable or that they even knew each other.

As historical works, *The Man in the Iron Mask* and Dumas' other books, are, at best, inaccurate; at worst, they are wholesale mutilations of the truth. Regardless, Dumas had the imaginative touch, the compulsion, and the intuitive gift to create personages and situations which, even in our own cynical times, have yet to lose their appeal and which, in his own day, made him France's bestselling author.

Not only for his readers, but also for himself, it is evident, Dumas' inventions—his fictions—seemed completely real. When his fabulous adventurers, The Three Musketeers, saved the king of France, imprisoned in a mask of iron, Dumas is said to have clapped his hands and rejoiced. On another occasion, Dumas' son, upon entering his father's study, found his father sobbing at his desk; nearly inconsolable, the author confessed that, with a stroke of his pen, he had just killed off Porthos, his favorite Musketeer.

From *Great Stories Behind Famous Books.* Copyright © 1999 by Don L. Wulffson. (Alleyside Press, 1999)

Student Assignment

Critical and Comparative Thinking

The reading selection provides a brief retelling of *The Man in the Iron Mask*. However, the presentation is closer to one of the many cinematic renderings of the story, one in which we see the horrendous ordeal of the twin, of his entry into the fetid prison, the locking of his head in the iron mask, and then his isolation and torment. Such a sequence is not to be found in Dumas' book; in reality, it begins with the prisoner already masked and a plot underway to free him.

Questions:

1. Why do you think the author chose such a presentation?

2. In the selection it mentions that "scholars wince at the liberties" Dumas took. Did the author of the selection take similar liberties? And if so, was he justified in doing so?

3. It might be said that the author of the selection "The Man In The Velvet Mask" did a disservice to his readers by adopting the presentation he did? Discuss.

4. For what reason(s), if any, are you now being alerted to the differences between the book and its rather deceptive presentation?

5. List at least three historical inaccuracies in *The Man in the Iron Mask*. Explain why you believe Dumas not only permitted them but presumably preferred these untruths and half-truths.

Point of View

The term "point of view" refers to the author's stance in relation to his story and characters. Primarily, the author can adopt either a *first person* or *third person* point of view.

First Person—The author is *inside* the story; he is one of the characters and freely refers to himself (using pronouns such as I, me, my, we, our, myself). For example: Gathering my willpower, I took my first few steps onto the bridge. Though it bounced with each step I took, it nevertheless seemed fairly solid. Wanting to get the terrifying ordeal over with as quickly as I could, I hurried along…

Third Person—The author is *outside* the story; he is *not* one of the characters and *never refers to himself.* For example: Gathering his willpower, Munson took his first few steps onto the bridge. Though it bounced with each step he took, it nevertheless seemed fairly solid. Wanting to get the terrifying ordeal over with as quickly as he could, he hurried along …

The following excerpt is from *The Man in the Iron Mask*:

> The door closed, leaving the King more astounded, more wretched, and more isolated than he had previously been. It was useless, though he tried it, to make the same noise as he had before on his door, and equally useless that he threw the plates and dishes out of his window; not a single sound was heard in answer, and the silence was torture to the King. He had only himself to turn to for solace; that is, he had none, further stirring the demons of torment in his mind. Two hours afterwards he could not be recognized as a king, a gentleman, a man, a human being; he might rather, be called a madman, tearing the door with his nails, trying to tear up the flooring of his cell, and uttering such wild and fearful cries that the old Bastille seemed to tremble in soundless trepidation at his shrieking lamentations.

1. The excerpt above is written from a third-person point of view. By simply changing the nouns and pronouns, transform it into the first-person. For example:

> The door closed, leaving the King more astounded, more wretched, and more isolated than he previously had been…

From *Great Stories Behind Famous Books.* Copyright © 1999 by Don L. Wulffson. (Alleyside Press, 1999)

2. Compare the two points of view in terms of the effect they have on you (both as a reader and as a writer). What are the strengths of each point of view? What are the weaknesses (or limitations)?

People Words

The reigning king in this selection is described as *sadistic*, meaning "to achieve pleasure from the infliction of pain on others." The word, as you may know, derives from the name of the French Marquis de Sade, who was known for this aberration.

Many other common words also derive from people's names. Using a dictionary and encyclopedia, give: (1) The meaning of each word below; and (2) The full name of the person from which the word derived.

1. braille

2. derrick

3. leotard

4. saxophone

5. guillotine

6. dahlia

7. guppy

8. sideburns

9. pompadour

10. silhouette

Writing

1. Write a paragraph which begins with the following topic sentence:

Alexander Dumas' Book *The Man in the Iron Mask* is historically inaccurate in a number of ways.

Use at least three supporting sentences following this topic sentence. (To assist you in writing your paragraph, refer to your response to question number 5 above under the rubric Critical and Comparative Thinking.

2. From a first-person point of view, write a true story from your own life that the word *anger* brings to mind.

3. Rewrite the story from a third-person point of view. Give a fictitious name for yourself.

Library and Information-Seeking Skills

1. Who was the King of France at the time in which the novel takes place? What kind of ruler was he? What were the conditions of the general populace at the time? Was the king's reign unique in any way, or not? During what years did that king reign?

2. Check biographical sources, encyclopedias, or author sources to find information on Alexander Dumas. Write a paragraph about his life, including the titles of his major writings.

Teacher Resources
Whole Language Activities for
"The Man in the Black Velvet Mask"

Before Reading Activities

Show a film (or video) version of *The Man in the Iron Mask*.

During Reading Activities

1. Have students read the selection silently. As they do, have them write down (or underline) any words that are unfamiliar to them.

2. Put a transparency of the selection on an overhead projector. Read it aloud; and after finishing each paragraph, call on students to identify the words they did not know. Underline these on the transparency; have students use context clues, dictionaries, and thesauruses to determine the words' meanings; next, have them suggest synonyms (or synonymous phrasing) for the words. Write these on the transparency as students create a glossary of the words.

After Reading Activities
Critical and Comparative Thinking

[Exercise sheet □]

The overall objective here is to encourage the students not to "believe everything they read." They need to learn how to read with a critical eye. At the same time, as readers, they should be alert to the author's purpose. Thus, though a technique may be suspect and a presentation deceptive, even fallacious, we still must make some allowance for the author's needs, his purpose—which, overall, is to create an effective piece of writing.

Point of View [Exercise sheet □]

As readers, students should (as a matter of routine) be aware of the author's point of view. If so desired, discuss point of view in more detail. That is: limited omniscient (third-person limited); omniscient (third-person unlimited); objective (dramatic). Too, point of view can be considered in terms of the author's purpose. This can be achieved by presenting two pieces of

writing, each from a different point of view, and discussing with the students how the "narrative angle" chosen by the author served specific needs.

People Words [Exercise sheet □]

Just as in the reading selections we probe the background of authors and their works, etymological activities such as "People Words" promote the students' awareness of the background (and evolution) of the words they daily encounter.

Writing [Exercise sheet □]

1. Promoting the development of skill in writing the "3-sentence paragraph" should be undertaken on a regular basis. Thus, this writing form is as appropriate to other reading selections as it is to "The Man in the Black Velvet Mask." Moreover, the writing need not be undertaken contemporaneously with the study of a particular chapter; for example, it can be used to reinforce the student's understanding and memory of previous selections.

2&3. Writing the personal narrative is an activity to which students take readily. In rewriting a narrative from a third-person point of view, the student discovers the process by which true-life experiences can be rendered into fiction.

Library and Information-Seeking Skills
[Exercise sheet □]

1. The best resource for answering the first question is a general history of France with a good index. If there are relatively few histories on this era in the library, refer the students to a good electronic encyclopedia.

2. Again, the best resource to learn about Alexander Dumas is a biography or a collected biography such as *World Authors* with a good index. There are also a number of good websites on Dumas that can be located using a browser.

From *Great Stories Behind Famous Books*. Copyright © 1999 by Don L. Wulffson. (Alleyside Press, 1999)

Chapter 14

A Man and A Woman of Letters

Hawthorne

Since it was first published in 1850, *The Scarlet Letter* has never been out of print, out of vogue with the public, nor out of favor with literary critics. In listings of the ten greatest American novels, it is invariably included; in any discussion of Nathaniel Hawthorne, one would be on extremely tenuous ground to disagree that it is by far his best work.

The story:

When she was young, Hester Prynne's family had married her to an elderly scholar. After living with her husband for some years in Antwerp, Belgium, she was sent alone across the Atlantic to Colonial America, the plan being that he would shortly follow. There had been news of his departure, but his ship had never been heard of again. Hester, young and attractive, after living alone in Boston for a considerable time, and believing herself to be a widow, had an affair, and consequently gave birth to a little girl, whom she named Pearl.

When news came that her husband was alive, Hester was found guilty of adultery by a court of stern Puritan judges. Her sentence: Including prison, she was condemned to wear on the breast of her gown a scarlet letter A, for adulteress. Then, to further humiliate her, for three hours, her baby Pearl in her arms, she was made to stand on the scaffold of the pillory before the townspeople of Colonial Boston.

Hester bore her shame openly and alone.

The father of the child did not come forward—and even when the ministers of the town, including the Reverend Arthur Dimmesdale, called upon her to reveal the man's identity, she declined. Shortly, she found herself keeping another secret: To her astonishment, as she stood on the scaffold, she spotted her elderly, now seemingly deformed-looking, husband standing at the edge of the woods. Like the father of her child, he did not come forward; not wanting it known he had been cuckolded, he put a finger to his lips as a signal for her to say nothing.

After her ordeal in the town square, Hester was returned to prison. There, in private, she was confronted by her husband, who told her that his ship had been wrecked on the coast; he had been injured and had been held captive among Indians for many months. Having taken the name Chillingworth to conceal his identity, he demanded that Hester not reveal his relationship to her, and she agreed not to do so. However, in a subtly ironic twist, hypocritically, he then demanded that she identify the father of her child; but to protect the man, coward though he might be, she refused.

After her release from jail, Hester found a small house on the outskirts of town; there, with her daughter Pearl, she settled down and earned a living doing needlework—and to her fellows offered only kindness, understanding, and love, tending to the ill and giving to the needy. Meanwhile, Dimmesdale grew increasingly ill, as though consumed by some inner disease—guilt; and slowly, in Chillingworth, grew the suspicion that Dimmesdale had been Hester's lover. Suspicion became conviction; Chillingworth then began taking sadistic pleasure in tormenting and further enfeebling the already ailing man.

Finally, consumed—morally, emotionally, and physically—by his cowardice and hypocrisy, the

Reverend Dimmesdale took Hester and Pearl by the hand, ascended the pillory, and admitted his guilt to the aghast townspeople. Then, dying, he sank to his knees.

Chillingworth, no longer able to wreak vengeance on Dimmesdale, died within the year. Cruel, cowardly, vengeful, he achieved some redemption of sin by bequeathing his considerable property to Pearl.

Hester continued on as before, living alone and wearing the scarlet letter on her breast. Beautifully, it is an emblem of her honesty; ironically, and again beautifully, it is a symbol of her ableness, and of her tenderness, understanding, and goodness of heart.

That, briefly, is the story.

And then there is another story, an even more intricate one: a complex admixture of influences which created a man who then created the story—the rarest of things, a masterpiece of literature.

Without Nathaniel Hawthorne, the book would never have come to be. Within his life we find all the pieces of the book—its setting, plot, characters, conflicts, and motifs. The book is a history of a sinister, darkly complex era of American history; and it is a reflection of the impact of that era upon the mind of one man, an artist who re-created it, seeking to give it shape and definition, and make it understandable—to himself and to his readers.

The Scarlet Letter is a profound examination of sin—or, really, of the consequences of sin, and of their subtle, insidious, and often convoluted workings upon the human soul. Sin—Hawthorne's preoccupation with it most assuredly sprang, at least in part, from his knowledge that two of his own ancestors had presided over the bloody persecutions during the Salem witchcraft trials. Stern, perverse Puritanical judges had nineteen innocent persons hanged for witchcraft, and one pressed to death.

And there was more of the same in his heritage: another incident, one which also took place in Salem. Among Hawthorne's ancestors of the seventeenth century were two sisters. Together they had to sit in the Salem meetinghouse with bands about their foreheads identifying their incestuous misconduct with

their brother. Branded, humiliated, and publicly shamed—as was the fictional Hester Prynne. As for their brother, one Captain Nicholas Manning, he hid in the woods—a coward, hiding, eluding punishment—as did the fictional Reverend Arthur Dimmesdale. And as did Chillingworth, standing there on the edge of the woods, a finger to his lips in a tacit demand for silence.

In his notebooks, Hawthorne wrote that he had long been tormented by this heritage of secret sin. Too, he mentioned a true tale once told him, the story of a Massachusetts woman whose punishment for adultery was to wear an A on her breast as an advertisement of her sinfulness. He would, he swore to himself, someday write a book using the incident as its basis.

The groundwork had been laid—the plot, setting, conflicts, theme. And then there came the characters; and it is legitimate to say that Nathaniel Hawthorne, in his fashion, was all of them; he had within himself all of the characters he brought to life on paper.

Pearl. The child was rambunctious, spirited, always up to something or other, such as climbing trees. Hawthorne was, at times, similarly free-spirited, sometimes mischievous, almost childish—especially when alone. Even in his adult years, he gamboled through the woods—and now and then climbed trees.

Pearl grew up without a father. So did Hawthorne; when he was only four, his father died at sea (and thus, like Chillingworth, never returned, never rejoined his family). Hawthorne well knew the void that Pearl felt.

Dimmesdale. Hawthorne, strangely, dressed as though he might be a minister. Usually, he wore black, with a high collar that partly veiled his face; at times, he wore a homemade New England approximation of a pontiff's robe. Too, like Dimmesdale, he was—especially in his writing—a sermonizer, a man seeking truth via the complex conduit of words. Yet he was laconic in his speaking; he rarely spoke, but when he did, using only a handful of words, he conveyed much.

Hawthorne was notoriously shy. He was known

to dart from the road into a nearby field when he spotted villagers approaching. When he went to social gatherings, it was always reluctantly; usually, he sat by himself, pensive, remote, brooding. Much like Dimmesdale, he was a man who lived secretly, afraid of what others might think of him; and surely, like his own character, to have come forward and revealed himself, and his private thoughts, would have been deathly painful.

And then there is the question of Hester Prynne. In *The Scarlet Letter*, Hawthorne captures the essence of her womanhood—her passion, her gentle strength, her capacity to mother, to succor, to nurture. How, one wonders, was a male able to render so artfully into words a female being?

The answer is quite simple: There was much about Hawthorne that was quite feminine. A gypsy woman once remarked upon seeing young Hawthorne: "Is that an angel? For a man was never so beautiful." A philosopher of the time commented in his journal that Hawthorne had "a voice that a woman might own, the hesitancy is so taking, and the tones so remote from what you expected." A painter, who once did a portrait of Hawthorne, observed: "I never had a young lady sit to me who was half so timid."

At other times, Hawthorne could be conspicuously manly—as though suddenly changing from one sort of being into another. One contemporary remarked that he was awed by Hawthorne, by "his voice so deep, with a weighty resounding quality."

Henry James found him to be "a bit crude" (like Chillingworth), and "looked like a rogue who suddenly finds himself in the company of detectives."

All of us have many sides to our personality, Hawthorne apparently more so than most. It seems he was many people agglomerated into one, and was capable of vividly projecting all of them—all of the characters in *The Scarlet Letter*: the impish, fatherless Pearl; the vulgar Chillingworth; the reticent, morose Dimmesdale; the wholly feminine—yet strong and capable—Hester Prynne.

Ultimately, Hawthorne was created by a complex variety of influences—his birthplace, his ancestors, his experiences, and the intricate inner-workings of his own multi-faceted personality. The latter included his talent, his gift of being able to look within himself and find the words to tell a story—both a powerful one and one he felt compelled to write. And finally there was his dedication to his work, his willingness to put aside all else and plunge wholly into the labor of artistic creation. During the process of writing *The Scarlet Letter*, in his wife's words, he wrote "immensely …. for many hours each day, in a kind of frenzy … vehemently, uninterested in all else, even his own health."

Writing the *The Scarlet Letter* took a toll on Hawthorne from which he never fully recovered, neither emotionally nor physically. He died in 1864, shortly after its completion.

From *Great Stories Behind Famous Books*. Copyright © 1999 by Don L. Wulffson. (Alleyside Press, 1999)

Student Assignment

Cooperative Learning

1. Write a ten-item quiz about "A Man and Woman of Letters." The quiz may be concerned with the development of any of the following reading skills: inferential thinking, fact versus opinion, cause and effect.

2. When you finish writing your quiz, exchange papers with a classmate. Write:

   Answered by __(your name)_____

   at the bottom of the paper.

3. When you finish answering the questions, again exchange papers. You and the other student then correct each other's work and turn it in to the teacher.

Critical and Comparative Thinking

1. In the writing of *The Scarlet Letter,* Hawthorne is considered by many to be a feminist, a spokesperson for women's rights. He opposed their oppression; he described and censured the underestimation of their multiple talents and strengths, which as often as not exceed those of men. Discuss.

2. What similarities, if any, do you see between *The Scarlet Letter* and the lives of the Bronte sisters?

3. Do you see any similarities between the lives of Hawthorne and Dickinson? What, if any, differences do you see?

4. Examine the title of the selection, "A Man and Woman of Letters."

   Is there any double meaning in it? How does the title relate to Hester Prynne? In what way(s), if at all, does it refer to Hawthorne?

5. Because of his father's death at sea, Hawthorne grew up dependent upon his mother. How is this fact of his childhood reflected in *The Scarlet Letter?*

6. Hawthorne knew the true story of a minister who, for mysterious reasons, wore a black veil; and in a story which predates *The Scarlet Letter,* wrote a fictional tale based on the man's life and his bizarre, unexplained veiling of himself. In what ways might this earlier work have influenced the content, characterization, and motifs of *The Scarlet Letter?*

7. Hawthorne's background was Puritan, a religion preoccupied with doing good and overcoming evil. Where—and by whom—is this tenet embraced in *The Scarlet Letter?*

8. Hawthorne's sister Elizabeth said that her brother had a "horror that his life would be written,"… and "it was his special injunction that no biography" of him ever be done. Despite his wishes, numerous biographies of the author have been published. In your opinion, was this wrong? In what ways, if any, can it be justified?

From *Great Stories Behind Famous Books.* Copyright © 1999 by Don L. Wulffson. (Alleyside Press, 1999)

Symbolism

The Scarlet Letter is a symbolical work. That is, many details represent more than they seem to on the surface; they suggest various concepts, truths, and motifs. For example, the little girl is named Pearl—and is, symbolically, "a gem of goodness" that issued from an otherwise negative, "sinful" episode. Based on "A Man and Woman of Letters," and the summary of the story it includes, answer the following questions to the best of your ability.

1. The scarlet letter is the central symbol of the story. For what does it stand early on? For what does it come to stand as the story evolves?

2. Colors are commonly used as standard, classic symbols. Perhaps especially in relation to a female, what does the color scarlet represent?

3. In the forest, Hawthorne describes sunlight as following Pearl and avoiding Hester. Symbolically, what is suggested here?

4. Hester emerges from the dark of the prison out into the light—and stands on the scaffold, not trying to hide anything about herself. Of what might darkness and light be symbolic here?

5. Outwardly, Chillingworth is physically deformed. What, possibly, might this suggest about his inner being?

6. Chillingworth is said to have had a reddish glow to his eyes. Of what might this be symbolic? Who—or what—else, even in our own time, is sometimes shown as having this same quality?

7. A rosebush grows near the door to the prison where Hester is incarcerated. Of what might this be a symbol?

8. The forest in which Hester lives is often described as dark and shadowy; at the same time, it is a place of many shades of green. Of what is green symbolic? How does green contrast and conflict with the symbolic darkness of the place?

Etymology: Places That Became Words

Hawthorne is described as a laconic man. The word laconic derives from the name of a place, Laconia, an ancient country situated near where Greece is today. Like laconic, the words below all came from place-names—towns, cities, countries, rivers, and mountains. The history of each word is given, as is its definition—but the letters of the words in each definition are scrambled. Unscramble them and write the definition(s) in the blanks.

Example:

Laconic—Named after the ancient country of Laconia.
spseerx ucmh isung wef sword
Express much using few words.

1. **Romance**—Named after Rome, Italy.

   eolv rfaafri ro vleo rysto

   _____

2. **Vaudeville**—Named after a valley in France, the Vau-de-vire, which was famous for light-hearted songs.

   gates hows fo dimex scat

   _____

3. **Turquoise**—So named because it was first brought to western Europe through Turkey.

   egm htta si lube ro regne ni ocrol

   _____

4. **Suede**—The French word for the country of Sweden.

   yetp fo elhtear hiwt het lhfse dise hnsuibdre nad ndtesfoe

   _____

5. *Afghan*—Named after the country of Afghanistan.

   fost pal tlkakne; sola, erebd fo uihtngn hudon

   _____

6. *Meander*—Named after the Menderes River in Turkey.

   ot awndre ro dwin nuaord

   _____

7. *Marathon*—On the fields of Marathon, greatly outnumbered Athenian troops defeated a Persian army; afterwards, a soldier ran 26 miles to bring news of the victory to Athens.

   na emteyxrel glon cfotoare ro rthoe teoctns ro tenve

   _____

8. *Stoic*—Named after the Stoa, a covered walkway in Athens, Greece.

   rsogtn dan alcm oerpsn htta skate het oogd tiwh teh dab; tefindifern ot nose now ospasin dan pina

   _____

9. *Bedlam*—Named after St. Mary of Bethlehem, a London mental hospital.

   na enaisn mlaysu; cicohat dna defcnous oaiutsitn

   _____

10. *Forum*—Named after the Forum, a public square in ancient Rome where legal and political business was conducted.

    na maseysbl lcpea; ocutr fo awl; ltuirbna

    _____

Writing

Read one of Hawthorne's short stories, then rewrite it as a play.

Consolidate the story; update the language a bit. Also, before you begin, study any play to get a better understanding of playwriting structure and technique.

As an example, the opening of *The Scarlet Letter* is redone below in dramatic form.

Narrator 1: It is a summer morning in Boston, in the early days of the Massachusetts Colony.

Narrator 2: A throng of people has gathered outside the jail, there to watch for Hester Prynne, who has been found guilty of adultery.

Old Woman 1: 'Tis my opinion that this hussy should be judged by women, and we would give a much harsher sentence than this.

Old Woman 2: They say that the Reverend Dimmesdale is very upset about the scandal.

Library and Information-Seeking Skills

1. Research Puritanism and describe its history. How did it evolve and from where? Are parts of it incorporated in today's American society, and if so, in what ways?

2. In what time period did Hawthorne live? Name other prominent New England authors that were Hawthorne's contemporaries and whom he may have known. In what ways were their styles and subjects different from Hawthorne? Use *The Reader's Companion to American History* or other print resource. Or try this (or another) literary research website:

   andromeda.rutgers.edu/~jlynch/Lit/american.html (Literary Resources—American).

3. Find three or more literary reference works about Hawthorne's life and writings. List the quantity and type of information you found in each source. Which would be the most informative and why? Does your library have any biographies of Hawthorne? (Remember, he did not want to have any written.) What other works did Hawthorne pen? Create a bibliography. Include the previous references at the end as "Resources."

From *Great Stories Behind Famous Books.* Copyright © 1999 by Don L. Wulffson. (Alleyside Press, 1999)

Teacher Resources
Whole Language Activities for "A Man and Woman of Letters"

Before Reading Activities

1. Show a film version of *The Scarlet Letter*.

2. Write the word *sin* on the board. Have students write their own personal definition of the word—what it means to them. Tell them to include a personal anecdote if they wish. Collect the papers; without giving names, read some of the papers aloud to the class.

During Reading Activities

1. Read "A Man and Woman of Letters" aloud to the class.

2. Have the students read *The Scarlet Letter* in its entirety.

3. Instruct students to read "A Man and Woman of Letters" again and then do the post-reading skills activities.

After Reading Activities

Cooperative Learning [Exercise sheet ☐]
The goal here is to continue to make young people active participants in the learning process (including assuming roles ordinarily the province of the teacher). Too, the activity reinforces the development and retention of reading skills previously addressed.

Critical and Comparative Thinking [Exercise sheet ☐]
"A Man and Woman of Letters" explores some aspects of Hawthorne's life and how they influenced his writing of *The Scarlet Letter*. The questions inculcate the student's ability to think deductively, inferentially, and conjecturally in analyzing details of his life presented in the selection—as well as details which were not presented in it and are probably new to them.

Symbolism [Exercise sheet ☐]
A basic understanding of symbolism—and being alert to its usage in any work—is an essential skill for all students of literature.

Explain the difference between standard symbols (e.g., light as truth) and symbols idiosyncratic to a specific work (e.g., Frost's "The Road Not Taken"). Tell students that some works, such as *The Scarlet Letter*, are highly symbolic, and recognizing and examining the symbols used is necessary to understanding the book. However, forewarn students not to "read in" symbolism where it does not exist (e.g., a light on in a house is not necessarily symbolic—that is, in most contexts, it is just a light).

Etymology: Places That Became Words
[Exercise sheet ☐]
Just as this book asks students to look for the "stories behind stories," the activities concerned with etymology alert them to the "stories behind words."

Answers:

1. Love affair or love story.

2. Stage show of mixed acts.

3. Gem that is blue or green in color.

4. Type of leather with the flesh side burnished and softened.

5. Soft lap blanket. Also, breed of hunting hound.

6. To wander or wind around.

7. An extremely long footrace or other contest or event.

8. Strong and calm person that takes the good with the bad; indifferent to ones own passion and pain.

9. An insane asylum; chaotic and confused situation.

10. An assembly place; court of law; tribunal.

From *Great Stories Behind Famous Books*. Copyright © 1999 by Don L. Wulffson. (Alleyside Press, 1999)

Supplemental Activity: Explain that many words are also derived from myths; for example, *morphine* from *Morpheus*, the Greek god of dreams. For each of the words below, have students give:

1. Its meaning;

2. The mythological figure from which it derives;

3. An explanation of the relationship between the word's meaning and its etymology.

1. tantalize	6. chaos
2. museum	7. lethargic
3. helium	8. odyssey
4. somnambulism	9. titanic
5. aphrodisiac	10. mercurial

Library and Information-Seeking Skills

[Exercise sheet ☐]

1. Either a print or CD-ROM encyclopedia will provide students with a start, but encourage them to go beyond these standard resources. For example, if the library has *Humanities Abstracts Full Text*, a Wilson database, it will provide in-depth background.

2. In addition to *The Reader's Companion to American History* and the website, recommend *World Authors: 800 BC–Present*, another commonly available Wilson publication.

3. Suggest one of the online bookstore databases such as www.Amazon.com **or** www.bn.com as the starting point in the students' search for books on Hawthorne.

From *Great Stories Behind Famous Books.* Copyright © 1999 by Don L. Wulffson. (Alleyside Press, 1999)

Further Reading

1. Madman On an Island

Defoe, Daniel. **Robinson Crusoe.** New American Library, 1960. To read *Robinson Crusoe,* naturally, is the initial step to understanding Defoe and his masterpiece, as it is to having a basis of comparison with other works embracing the specific motifs and general story-line and scenario of the castaway.

Golding, William. **Lord of the Flies.** Faber & Faber, 1954. The ultimate story derived from the castaway scenario, an allegory in which children are escaping a nuclear holocaust. When their plane crashes, they find themselves re-enacting the primordial horrors of human behavior on an Edenesque island. The Lord of the Flies, Golding is saying, is the sub-bestial devil inherent in all of us and to which we are driven to pay homage.

Heyerdahl, Thor. **Fatu-Hiva: Back to Nature.** Doubleday & Company, 1975. A twentieth-century Robinson Crusoe, the youthful Thor Heyerdahl spent the year 1936 with his bride, Liv, on Fatu-Hivva in the primitive Marquesas Islands. Undecided about their future, the Heyerdahls wanted to escape civilization and live strictly according to nature. They find paradise, and the natural serenity they were seeking; and then they find horror: with no medical supplies, and lacking civilization's devices for surviving the insidious dangers and ugliness of nature, they come within inches of losing their lives.

Knowles, Josiah N. **Crusoes of Pitcairn Island.** Dawson Books, 1957. This is a detailed diary of Captain Knowles who, in 1858, was shipwrecked on Oeno Atoll in the Pacific. Though lacking the true storyteller's touch with words, this work, as with other true accounts of the same ilk, nevertheless lends insight into the reality confronting the castaway.

Neider, Charles, ed. **Great Shipwrecks and Castaways.** Harper and Brothers, 1952. A highly interesting collection of true accounts of the experiences of castaways. More readable than the Knowles' book, it also proffers a more comprehensive understanding of the plight of those who have confronted the awesome power of the sea and the numbing prospect of being marooned, either alone or in the company of others.

Verne, Jules. **The Mysterious Island.** TOR, 1995. In 1865, a hot-air balloon carrying five persons escaping the Confederacy during the Civil War falls into the sea near a strange, uncharted island. Primarily, this is a story of survival and a celebration of the adaptability and ingenuity of humankind. A wealth of description and scientific detail and convincing explanations of mysterious happenings lend the work texture, depth, and a sense of realism.

Wulffson, Don. **The Upside-Down Ship.** Whitman, 1986. In this novelization of a true event, Bruce Gordon, the only survivor of a sea disaster, lives for seven years in an upside-down ship that has become frozen and embedded in an Arctic iceberg.

2. A Person in Two

Kafka, Franz. "The Metamorphosis," in **The Penal Colony: Stories and Short Pieces.** Schocken, 1948. A horror story of profound depth and meticulous texturing, "Metamorphosis" tells of Gregor Samsa who awakens one morning to find himself transformed in his bed into a gigantic insect. As Stevenson dealt with the dark side of the self, Kafka, in this story and others, probes modern man's alienation from himself, a slow self-rendering and departure from that which one would like to be into something foreign and detestable.

Griffin, John. ***Black Like Me.*** New American Library, 1960. Caucasian author John Howard Griffin, his skin temporarily darkened by medical treatments, hair shaved, crosses the "color line," and passes as an African American in the Deep South. In this masterful, shocking true-life narrative, the author experiences squalor, violence, bigotry, and injustice; in short, he endures the horror which far too long has been the lot of African Americans, which only now has begun to be understood and extirpated.

Sparks, Christine. ***The Elephant Man.*** Ballantine, 1980. The remarkable true story of John Merrick—a good, gentle, and intelligent man—imprisoned in the body of a monster. As with the other works recommended here, this work enables us to continue our investigation into the duality of man, of the two-sidedness of us all. As Stevenson explores the good and evil inherent in each of us, Ms. Sparks' work is gripping testimony to the complex unity, interaction, and indivisibility of the ugliness and beauty of us all.

Wilde, Oscar. ***The Picture of Dorian Gray.*** Random House, 1992. Once again, we embrace the duality of man—here, that of the complex interfacing of youth and age (too, of the complex duplicity of the moral and immoral). In the work, Dorian is saddened at the sight of his just-completed portrait: He would become old and wrinkled, while the picture would remain the same. He wishes, instead, that the portrait might grow old while he remained forever young. In this state of mind, he is thus prompted to say he would give his soul to keep his youth—which he does.

3. Will You Marry Me, Alice in Wonderland?

Carroll, Lewis. ***Alice's Adventures in Wonderland & Through the Looking Glass.*** Bantam, 1988. Only in reading *Alice in Wonderland* do we begin to appreciate its compelling charm and power. And then there is *Through the Looking Glass*; it is a rare thing: a sequel which is as good as, if not better than, the book which preceded it. Like *Alice's Adventures in Wonderland*, it is peopled with strange creatures; and it is more. Carroll planned it in the form of a chess problem, and Alice turns out to be a White Pawn who wins a bizarre yet wonderfully enjoyable game.

Carroll, Lewis. "Jabberwocky," ***The Norton Anthology of English Literature, Vol. II.*** W.W. Norton. "Jabberwocky" is perhaps the finest example of the English tradition of nonsense verse, pleasurable to read on its most surface

level, exquisitely profound when plumbed at deeper levels (e.g., its parodying of the heroic and the martial). The poem exhibits a mathematician's fondness for puzzles combined with a literary man's fondness for word games; and more, it is a key to understanding the nonsense of which life is often made, and of the edifying nonsense that is the stuff of Carroll's work.

Hinde, Thomas. ***Lewis Carroll, Looking-Glass Letters.*** Rizzoli, 1992. Carroll wrote thousands of letters to his family, friends and colleagues, a handful of the most intriguing of which are contained in this exceptional work. There are joking, nonsense letters to Alice Liddell, deferential letters to eminent contemporaries such as Tennyson and Rossetti, and letters of detailed instruction to his illustrator, Tenniel. Paintings, sketches, cartoons and photographs—some taken by Carroll himself—combine with the letters to create a profound, haunting picture of the workings of Carroll's mind and of the times in which he lived.

Tolkien, J.R.R. ***The Hobbit*** and ***The Lord of the Rings.*** Houghton Mifflin, 1955. As with Carroll's work, those of Tolkein are organized around the idea of a journey into the unknown and back again, making the stories circular in form. Again, as with Carroll, underpinning the whimsy, fantasy, and nonsense, are serious themes such as: responsible use of power; common people versus the elite; the importance of friendship; and the nature of heroism. Those who find themselves endeared of the works of Carroll will readily discover in Tolkein a continuation of his predecessor's peculiar magic.

4. Vlad Tepes: The Real Dracula

Stoker, Bram. ***Dracula.*** TOR, 1988.

Bunson, Matthew. ***The Vampire Encyclopedia.*** Crown, 1993. An informative and accessible work covering everything from vampire history to the psychology of vampires.

Fanu, J. Sheridan Le. ***Carmilla.*** Gaverston, 1872. The Countess Mircalla Karnstein is considered by many to be the female equivalent of Count Dracula in terms of influence on vampire literature, and there can be little doubt that Stoker was influenced by this short novel.

King, Stephen. ***Salem's Lot.*** Dutton, 1975. The King of Horror tells of Kurt Barlow, an ancient vampire who moves into the small town of Jerusalem's Lot, and proceeds to go into a feeding (and blood-drinking) frenzy. In lurid detail, the author describes how this once pleasant town is slowly transformed into a colony of vampires. Ultimately, the protagonists cleanse the town of vampires through fire—though the ending leaves the reader wondering if they have succeeded.

Marigny, Jean. *Vampires: The World of the Undead.* Thames and Hudson, 1994. A brief but thorough examination of the vampire myth.

Matheson, Richard. *I Am Legend.* Dell, 1954. Sci-fi and vampirism are brought together in this chilling work, which was so popular it was twice made into movies, "The Last Man on Earth" (1964) and "The Omega Man (1971), the latter of which is available on video. The storyline: A plague has killed most of the people on Earth, and all the survivors have turned into vampires, except for one man, the protagonist, who spends his days hunting and killing the bloodthirsty monsters.

McNally, Raymond. *In Search of Dracula.* Houghton Mifflin,1994. Updated and revised from a 1972 edition, the work is a compelling and highly informative examination of the life of Vlad Tepes and the genesis of the Dracula myth.

Page, Carol. *Bloodlust.* Dell, 1991. A highly interesting but disturbing collection of interviews with real-life vampires.

Polidori, John. "The Vampyre," (1819). It is evident from Stoker's journals and diaries that *Dracula* was influenced by several earlier works, among them this short story. Intriguingly, Polidori, you may recall, was amongst the group of travelers in Geneva with whom Mary Shelley stayed while writing *Frankenstein.*

Rice, Ann. *Interview with the Vampire.* Knopf, 1976. The reader is introduced in this work to perhaps the most popular vampire of recent literature, Lestat de Lioncourt. We learn more about Lestat in the author's Vampire Chronicles series, which includes *The Vampire Lestat, The Queen of the Damned,* and *The Tale of the Body Thief.*

Wolf, Leonard. *The Essential Dracula.* Plume, 1993. This annotated version of Stoker's novel is crammed with fascinating information, the footnotes being as intriguing to read as the novel.

5. The Genius

Bronte, Charlotte. *Jane Eyre.* Oxford University Press, 1975. In this superb work, in both heroine and hero, the author introduced character types wholly new to English fiction. Jane, a shy, intense orphan, never for a moment displays those qualities of superficial beauty and charm that had marked the conventional heroine. Edward Rochester, Jane's lover, is a strange, violent man, bereft of conventional courtesy, who lives by a law unto himself. The bond of love between the two is, in part, a bond of mutual pain; and that which keeps them apart is a shared darkness, a shared horror: unearthly shrieking and laughter that come from the mansion's attic late at night.

Bronte, Emily. *Wuthering Heights.* Oxford University Press, 1975. Again, the protagonists are at odds with the conventions of characterization typical of nineteenth-century literature. The hero is a strange, uncouth passionate creature named Heathcliff, who grows up with Hindley and Catherine Earnshaw in their lonely moorland home (reminiscent of the author's places of upbringing, as well as her sisters'). Heathcliff's love is terrifying; and when Catherine, though she returns his love, marries Edgar Linton, his thwarted passion finds sinister outlet against the Lintons and Earnshaws of his own and the succeeding generation.

Eliot, George. various works   The life and works of Mary Ann Evans, who wrote under the male pseudonym George Eliot, parallel and illuminate the times, frustrations, and writings of the Bronte sisters. Ms. Eliot's works include *Scenes from Clerical Life* (1857); *Adam Bede* (1859); *The Mill on the Floss* (1860); *Silas Marner* (1861); *Romola* (1863); *Felix Holt* (1866); *Middlemarch* (1872). Eliot is known for her scholarly accomplishments, her intellectual power, her studies of character, and her treatment of social problems. During her lifetime, she was widely criticized for her opposition to organized religion, the conventions of marriage, and her espousal of women's rights.

Fraser, Rebecca Fraser. *The Brontes: Charlotte Bronte and Her Family.* Ballantine Books, 1988. Writing from a contemporary perspective and drawing on previously unknown documents, Fraser's biographical work is worthy of its subject, combining a social historian's sense of place and a novelist's imaginative feeling for detail.

Gardiner, Juliet. *The Brontes at Haworth: The World Within.* Clarkson Potter, 1992. This is the story both of the real world of the Brontes at Haworth Parsonage, their home on the edge of the lonely Yorkshire moors, and of the imaginary worlds they spun for themselves.

Further illuminating the lives of the sisters are rarely seen examples of their talents as painters.

6. The Birth of Frankenstein
Shelley, Mary. *Frankenstein*. Pocket Books, 1995.

◦◦◦

Butler, Octavia E. *Parable of the Sower.* Four Walls Eight Windows. During the twenty-first century, California is devastated by supernatural disasters. An African American teenager emerges as a prophet of "Earthseed," a new religion, the prime tenet of which is that humankind must emigrate, with reverence, to the stars.

Bradbury, Ray. *Fahrenheit 451.* Ballantine, 1953. The title *Fahrenheit 451* is a stroke of genius, being the temperature at which paper spontaneously ignites. The hero, who repents of his book-burning job as a "fireman" in totalitarian America, begins instead to memorize literary works in the company of other rebels, thereby preserving the past as well as our hope for the future.

Cook, Robin. *Coma.* New American Library, 1977. When dozens of patients are admitted to Memorial Hospital for routine procedures, all fall prey to the same inexplicable, hideous tragedy on the operating table: None ever awakens. Some traceless error in anesthesia has caused irreversible brain death, leaving each in a hopeless coma. The heroine, a young medical student, hazards her life to uncover a plot that is ghastly, nightmarishly possible, and firmly rooted in Frankensteinian tradition.

Kapec, Karel. *R.U.R. (Rossum's Universal Robots).* Czechoslovakia: Vydalo Aventinum, 1923. This play introduced the word "robot" (suggested by Karel's brother Josef) to the world. It is Czech for "worker," and Kapek's robots are, in fact, what we now would call androids, created as industrial slaves. They revolt; the play ends—in chaos, with a touch of hope.

Heinlein, Robert. *Starship Troopers.* Putnam, 1959. Originally written (and rejected by Scribners) as a young adult book, Putnam took it as an adult item—which it is. *Starship Troopers* traces the coming of age of a cadet who learns to be a warrior for just the kind of conflict which, to our horror, Vietnam (right around the corner) turned out to be. Is it satire or the author's true goal when Heinlein puts his foot down against liberal values? He seems to be saying that questioning Honor and Duty is poisonous, and saps the manhood of a boy. Or, is he saying something else altogether?

Orwell, George. *1984.* Secker and Warburg, 1949. The world of 1984 is one in which eternal warfare is the price of bleak prosperity, in which The Party keeps itself in power by complete control over human actions and thoughts. As the lovers Winston Smith and Julia learn when they try to evade the Thought Police, and then join the underground opposition, the Party can smash the last impulse of love, the last flicker of individuality.

Wells, H.G. *The War of the Worlds.* Heinemann, 1898. Wells's Martians land in saucer-shaped spacecraft that cut great furrows in the countryside. Their weapons are ominous and the destruction terrifying. When, ultimately, they are killed, it is not our impotent guns that save our hides, but our germs.

7. Night of Futility
Lord, Walter. *A Night to Remember.* Bantam Books, 1978. (Illustrated edition.) When, in 1912, the "unsinkable" *Titanic* sank with appalling loss of life, it was one of the great news stories of all time. However, the tragedy was little more than a distant haunting memory, when Walter Lord's *A Night to Remember* first appeared in print in 1955. The gripping bestseller introduced the drama to a whole new generation of readers as well as being the stimulus to unprecedented historical and scientific examination of the vessel and the event.

◦◦◦

Gardner, Martin. *The Wreck of the Titanic Foretold.* Prometheus Books, 1986. Morgan Robertson's apparently prophetic sea novel, *The Wreck of the Titan*, is reproduced in this work in full, along with a selection of other writings that seem to foretell the *Titanic*'s fate. Only by reading Robertson's actual work can one judge the degree to which the work actually predicts a future occurrence and the degree to which those with an eye to sensationalism have capitalized upon the coincidental.

Hoehling, A.A. *Great Ship Disasters.* Cowles, 1971. The *Andrea Doria–Stockholm* collision, the tragic sinking of the *General Slocum*, the firestorm aboard the *Morro Castle*, and the mystery-laden torpedoing of the *Lusitania* are but a few of the oceanic disasters studied in this compendium.

Lord, Walter. *The Night Lives On.* William Morrow, 1986. In the years since the publication of *A Night to*

Remember, Lord has continued his research into every aspect of the story of the *Titanic*, and the result is this fascinating companion volume that explores many of the riddles that have long puzzled both the experts and the public: How well built was the "unsinkable" *Titanic*? Did the captain really know how to handle the ship? Why were six wireless warnings ignored? Who was responsible for there being so few lifeboats? What was the band really playing? Why weren't *Titanic*'s rockets answered? And finally, now that she has been found, what are the chances of salvaging the *Titanic*?

Shaw, Frank. *Full Fathom Five*. MacMillan, 1930. This work provides fairly detailed accountings of several other sinkings, each of which was unique and makes for compelling reading.

Watson, Milton. *Disasters at Sea*. Patrick Stephens, 1987. The popular media has left us with the impression that the sinking of the *Titanic* was perhaps the only loss of an ocean-going liner of genuine interest and importance. *Disasters at Sea* chronicles the essential events surrounding the loss of every passenger liner since 1900, and provides a fine sourcebook for further study of other sinkings of particular interest to the reader.

8. Of Mice and Men

Steinbeck, John. *Of Mice and Men*. Covici Friede Publishers, 1937.

Benson, Jackson. *The True Adventures of John Steinbeck*. Penguin, 1984. Benson's work is perhaps the definitive biography of Steinbeck. Rich in detail, in anecdote, in literary criticism, this omnibus plumbs the life of Steinbeck with great feeling for emotional nuance and historical precision.

Sinclair, Upton. *The Jungle*. New American Library, 1960. As is Steinbeck, Upton Sinclair is a powerful spokesperson for the rights of the working man, and for freedom, equality, and humanity. In *The Jungle*, in some of the most harrowing scenes ever written in modern literature, Sinclair vividly depicts the horror of the slaughterhouses in Chicago in the first years of the twentieth century. The venue is different from that of any of Steinbeck's works, and Sinclair's voice is less modulated and more openly outraged; nevertheless, to embrace the message of either author is to begin to comprehend them both.

Steinbeck, John. *The Grapes of Wrath*. Viking Penguin Publications, 1939. This Pulitzer-Prize-winning book is perhaps the standard-bearer of American proletarian literature, that sub-genre which has as its aim a sympathetic portrayal of the lives and sufferings of the "common man" and an exposure of the injustices of the society in which they live, with a view toward inducing amelioration. *The Grapes of Wrath* tells of the hardships of the Joad family, farmers who are leaving the Oklahoma Dust Bowl region for California in search of work, only to confront blatant as well as insidious social injustice—by which the family is defeated yet remains resolute in its determination to ultimately overcome, if not destroy.

————. *In Dubious Battle*. Viking Penguin Publications, 1939. A precursor to *The Grapes of Wrath*, the work deals with labor organization among migrant fruit-pickers in California. Strikes, violence by the local vigilantes, and the murder of a young Communist leader, are featured. Though less ambitious in scope and characterization than *The Grapes of Wrath*, the work nonetheless is a full-bodied story; and there is in the word "dubious" (in the title) a suggestion of the ambiguity and questionable worthiness of all social causes, no matter how meritorious and pure they may outwardly appear.

————. *Tortilla Flat*. Penguin, 1985. This work offers us a different perspective on Steinbeck, on that side of him which allowed him to shrug off tragedy with a smile and enjoy the humor—silliness!—inevitably to be found in our daily comings and goings through life. Tortilla Flat, a shabby district above the town of Monterey, California, is home to a misguided, easy-going, colorful gang partaking of meaningless revels while residing in idyllic poverty.

9. The Woman in White

Benfey, Christopher. *Emily Dickinson: Lives of a Poet*. George Braziller. Benfey provides an in-depth but highly readable and enjoyable look into the life and poetry of Dickinson. Readers will especially appreciate the photographs as they will the author's unintimidating style combined with the completeness of his portraiture.

Bloom, Harold, ed. *Emily Dickinson*. Chelsea House, 1985. This work proffers a complete critical portrait, and contains essays on Dickinson's works by numerous highly respected scholars. The essays, reprinted in the order of their publication, provide an absorbing chronicle of modern critical responses to the subtlety of Emily Dickinson's poetry.

Linscott, Robert, ed. *Selected Poems & Letters of Emily Dickinson*. Doubleday Anchor, 1959. A superb collection of some many of the finest of Ms. Dickinson's writings. Her letters are especially helpful in illuminating idiosyncrasies of the mind and life of this most elusive of artists

Moore, Christopher, ed. *Emily Dickinson: Selected Poems*. Park Lane Press, 1993. To fathom the power and beauty and uniquity of Dickinson's work, the reader, of necessity, must begin with her poems, indulging in them in isolation and taking from them whatever is privately found. Mr. Moore's collection—his selection—is rarely beyond reproach.

10. To Look Death in the Eye

Amoia, Alba. *Feodor Dostoyevsky*. Ungar, 1993. Excellent biographical material and insightful critical studies of Dostoyevsky's short stories and novels as they pertain to the artist's world and to the world in which we live today.

Bloom, Harold. *Fyodor Dostoyevsky's Crime and Punishment*. Chelsea House, 1996. A better-than-average introduction to the life of Dostoyevsky, including a synopsis and thematic and structural analysis of *Crime and Punishment*.

Bloom, Harold, ed. *Fyodor Dostoyevsky*. Chelsea House, 1988. An in-depth look at the inter-relationship between the specifics of the man's life (his epilepsy, psychological difficulties, religion, ideology, etc.) and geneses of his works.

Dostoyevsky, Fyodor. *Notes from Underground*. Bantam Books, 1992. A splendid short novel in which the irascible voice of a nameless narrator cries out: "I am a sick man. I am a spiteful man." The passionate confessions and brutal self-examination of a tormented man, *Notes from Underground*, first published in 1864, presages the moral, political, and social ideas the artist treats on a monumental scale in *Crime and Punishment, The Idiot*, and *The Brothers Kramazov*.

11. To Stir a Curious Mind

Christie, Agatha. *An Autobiography*. Dodd, Mead, 1977. Ms. Christie began to write this book in 1950; she finished some twenty-five years later when she was 75 years old. The manuscript, as whole, as to be expected, contained some inconsistencies and repetitions, and

these have been minimalized under the watchful and sympathetic eye of her daughter Rosalind. Nothing of importance has been omitted, though she ended it when she was in her seventies, somewhat prematurely. As she put it: "It seems the right moment to stop… because [as far as I am concerned], there is nothing further to say."

———. *Ten Little Indians*. Pocket Books, 1939. This is an especially potent and spell-binding mystery. One by one, guests arrive at Indian Island, each summoned by a bizarre command. And one by one, with terrifying meticulousness, they are murdered. By whom? And why? Initially, there seems to be no pattern, until someone notices a nursery rhyme, framed and hung over the fireplace.

———. *Three Blind Mice*. Dodd, Mead, 1925. One of the prolific Ms. Christies' best, the legendary Hercule Poirot's powers are taxed to the limit as he grapples with a kidnapper so arrogant he announces his intentions beforehand, a murderer who leaves abundant clues, and an eccentric man who changes the habits of a lifetime… on the day before he "accidentally" plunges to his death. Poroit is joined by the disarmingly sweet Miss Marple in providing the ingenuity and suspense that has long distinguished Ms. Christie as a writer of mysteries without equal.

———. *The Witness for the Prosecution*. Berkley, 1984. Agatha Christie's most famous story, this classic courtroom drama was made into a play and filmed twice. It is the story of a young man on trial for murder in an open-and-shut case … when shocking new testimony turns the tables in one of the greatest surprise endings ever devised.

Tynan, Kathleen. *Agatha*. Ballantine, 1978. This work, with meticulous but sometimes suspect information, describes in detail, and in novel-like form, the entire story of Agatha Christie's mysterious disappearance.

Weinberg, Robert. *100 Dastardly Little Detective Stories*. Barnes & Noble, 1993. The short detective story has a venerable tradition that extends back to the very origins of detective fiction. The earliest story in this spine-tingling collection, Abraham Lincoln's "The Trailor Murder Mystery," appeared in 1843, and in the century-and-a-half since, the detective story has attracted the interest of some of the most distinguished names in fiction, including Charles Dickens, Jack London, Bret Hart, and the master of the short story, O. Henry. All of these writers are represented in *100 Dastardly Little Detective Stories*.

12. Diagnosis: Innocent

Doyle, Sir Arthur Conan. *The Complete Sherlock Holmes.* Doubleday, 1927. It is difficult to find a more complete or superb collection of Doyle's work: Contained in this volume are all four of Doyle's four full-length novels and 56 short stories about the colorful adventures of Sherlock Holmes—every word Conan Doyle ever wrote about Baker Street's most famous resident.

Cox, Don Richard. *Arthur Conan Doyle.* Frederick Ungard, 1985. Cox's volume provides rare insight into the life of Doyle and into the workings of his complex and intriguing mind. It is all here—Doyle's years as a doctor, his creation of Holmes, his embracing of spiritualism, and his fervent desire to be remembered as a first-rate historical novelist rather than "just a mere mystery writer."

13. The Man in the Black Velvet Mask

Dumas, Alexander. *The Man in the Iron Mask.* Oxford University Press, 1992.

Dumas, Alexander. *The Count of Monte Cristo.* Oxford University Press, 1990. Edmond Dantes, a sailor, falsely accused of treason, is arrested on his wedding day and imprisoned in an island fortress. After a dramatic escape, he sets out to wreak vengeance on his enemies, and at the same time, discover the fabulous treasure of Monte Cristo. A tale filled with great tension and excitement, *The Count of Monte Cristo* is also a fascinating look into the complex nature and sometimes twisted consequences of seeking revenge.

14. A Man and Woman of Letters

Hawthorne, Nathaniel. *The Scarlet Letter.* Vintage Books, 1990.

Bloom, Harold, ed. *Nathaniel Hawthorne's The Scarlet Letter: Interpretations.* Chelsea House, 1986.

Hawthorne, Nathaniel. *The House of the Seven Gables.* W.W. Norton, 1967.

Kazin, Alfred. *Selected Short Stories of Nathaniel Hawthorne.* Fawcett, 1996. This is perhaps the best collection of Hawthorne's tales for students to use when completing the playwriting activity following "A Man & Woman of Letters."

Leone, Bruno, et. al., eds. *Readings on Nathaniel Hawthorne.* Greenhaven, 1996. A superb collection of scholarly but highly readable essays by various critics, each of which offers a different perspective on the life and works of Hawthorne.

Miller, Edwin. *Salem Is My Dwelling Place: A Life of Nathaniel Hawthorne.* University of Iowa Press, 1991. An excellent work which provides an in-depth look into Hawthorne's life, intellect, and growth as a writer.

Pearson, Norman, ed. *The Complete Novels and Selected Tales of Nathaniel Hawthorne.* Modern Library, 1993. An exemplary collection of Hawthorne's best works.

Bibliography

Alba, Amoia. *Feodor Dostoevsky.* Ungar Books, 1993.

Benet, William. *The Reader's Encyclopedia.* Crowell, 1948.

Benfey, C. *Emily Dickinson.* Braziller, 1986.

Benson, J. *The Adventures of John Steinbeck.* Penguin, 1985.

Bloom, Harold. *The Brontes—Modern Critical Views.* Chelsea House, 1987.

———. *Emily Dickinson.* Chesea House, 1985.

———. *Fyodor Dostoevsky's Crime and Punishment.* Chelsea House, 1996.

Bradley Sculley. *The American Tradition in Literature.* Norton, 1962.

Brinton, Crane. *Modern Civilization.* Prentice-Hall, 1967.

Bronte, Charlotte. *Jane Eyre.* Oxford University Press, 1975.

Buckler, William. *Prose of the Victorian Period.* Houghton Mifflin, 1958.

Bunson, Matthew. *The Vampire Encyclopedia.* Crown, 1993.

Christie, Agatha. *An Autobiography.* Dodd, Mead, 1977.

Coleman, James. *Abnormal Psychology and Modern Life.* University of Chicago Press, 1956.

Defoe, Daniel. *Robinson Crusoe.* New American Library, 1960.

Encylopedia Britannica. Benton, 1972.

Fraser, Rebecca. *The Brontes.* Ballantine, 1988.

Gardiner, Juliet. *The Brontes at Haworth.* Clarkson Potter, 1992.

Gardner, M. *The Wreck of the Titanic Foretold.* Prometheus, 1986.

Griffin, John. *Black Like Me.* New American Library, 1960.

Heyerdahl, Thor. *Fatu-Hiva.* Doubleday, 1975.

Hinde, Thomas. *Lewis Carroll, Looking-Glass Letters.* Rizzoli, 1992.

Hoehling, A. *Great Ship Disasters.* Cowles, 1971.

Kafka, Franz. *The Penal Colony.* Schocken, 1948.

Lear, E. *Teapots and Quails and Other Nonsense.* Harvard University Press, 1953.

Le Fanu, J. *Carmilla.* Penseus, 1872.

Linscott, R. *Selected Poems & Letters of Emily Dickinson.* Doubleday, 1959.

Lord, Walter. *The Night Lives On.* Morrow, 1986.

———. *A Night to Remember.* Bantam, 1955.

McNally, Raymond T., and Radu Florescu. *In Search of Dracula.* Houghton Mifflin, 1994.

Marigny, J. *Vampires: The World of the Undead.* Thames and Hudson, 1994.

Neider, Charles. *Great Ships and Castaways.* Harper, 1952.

Norton Anthology of English Literature, Vol. II. Norton, 1962.

Page, Carol. *Bloodlust.* Dell, 1991.

Perkins, David. *English Romantic Writers.* Harcourt, Brace, 1967.

Perreine, Laurence. *Sound and Sense.* Harcourt, 1963

Shaw, Frank. *Full Fathom Five.* MacMillan, 1930.

Shelley, Mary. *Frankenstein.* Pocket Books, 1995.

Sinclair, Upton. *The Jungle.* New American Library, 1960.

Bibliography

Sparks, Christine. *The Elephant Man.* Ballantine, 1980.

Steinbeck, John. *Of Mice and Men.* Penguin, 1994.

Tynan, Kathleen. *Agatha.* Ballantine, 1978,

Untermeyer, B. & L. *Children's Literature.* Western, 1966.

Untermeyer, Louis. *Lives of the Poets.* Simon & Schuster, 1959.

Watson, Milton. *Disasters at Sea.* Patrick Stephens Books,

Welch, S. *Vampire Almanac.* Random House, 1995.

Wolf, L. *The Essential Dracula.* Plume, 1993.

Woods, George. *Poetry of the Victorian Period.* Scott, Foresman, 1955.